BIOLOGICAL ASPECTS OF DEMOGRAPHY

SOCIETY FOR THE STUDY OF HUMAN BIOLOGY

Although there are many scientific societies for the furtherance of the biological study of man as an individual, there has been no organization in Great Britain catering for those (such as physical anthropologists or human geneticists) concerned with the biology of human populations. The need for such an association was made clear at a Symposium at the Ciba Foundation in November 1957, on "The Scope of Physical Anthropology and Human Population Biology and their Place in Academic Studies". As a result the Society for the Study of Human Biology was founded on May 7th, 1958, at a meeting at the British Museum (Natural History).

The aims of the Society are to advance the study of the biology of human populations and of man as a species, in all its branches, particularly human variability, human genetics and evolution, human adaptability and ecology.

At present the Society holds two full-day meetings per year—a Symposium (usually in the autumn) on a particular theme with invited speakers, and a scientific meeting for proffered papers. The papers given at the Symposia are published and the monographs are available to members at reduced prices.

Persons are eligible for membership who work or who have worked in the field of human biology as defined in the aims of the Society. They must be proposed and seconded by members of the Society. The subscription is £3 ($7.00) per annum (this includes the Society's journal *Human Biology*) and there is no entrance fee.

Applications for membership should be made to Dr. W. A. Marshall, Hon. General Secretary, Institute of Child Health, Guilford St., London, W.C.1.

PUBLICATIONS OF THE SOCIETY

Symposia, Volume I, 1958: *The Scope of Physical Anthropology and Its Place in Academic Studies*, edited by D. F. ROBERTS and J. S. WEINER (out of print).

Symposia, Volume II, 1959: *Natural Selection in Human Populations*, edited by D. F. ROBERTS and G. A. HARRISON. Pergamon Press (£1).

Symposia, Volume III, 1960: *Human Growth*, edited by J. M. TANNER. Pergamon Press (members 10s. 6d.).

Symposia, Volume IV, 1961: *Genetic Variation in Human Populations*, edited by G. A. HARRISON. Pergamon Press (members £1).

Symposia, Volume V, 1963: *Dental Anthropology*, edited by D. R. BROTHWELL. Pergamon Press (members 25s.).

Symposia, Volume VI, 1964: *Teaching and Research in Human Biology*, edited by G. A. HARRISON. Pergamon Press (members 25s.).

Symposia, Volume VII, 1965: *Human Body Composition, Approaches and Applications*, edited by J. BROZEK. Pergamon Press (members £3).

Symposia, Volume VIII, 1968: *The Skeletal Biology of Earlier Human Populations*, edited by D. R. BROTHWELL. Pergamon Press (members £2.).

Symposia, Volume IX, 1969: *Human Ecology in the Tropics*, edited by J. P. GARLICK and R. W. J. KEAY. Pergamon Press (members 30s.).

SYMPOSIA OF THE
SOCIETY FOR THE STUDY OF HUMAN BIOLOGY

Volume X

BIOLOGICAL ASPECTS OF DEMOGRAPHY

Edited by

W. BRASS

TAYLOR & FRANCIS LTD

London

1971

First published 1971 by Taylor & Francis Ltd, 10–14 Macklin Street,
London WC2B 5NF

© 1971 Taylor & Francis Ltd

Printed and bound in Great Britain by Taylor and Francis Ltd,
10–14 Macklin Street, London WC2B 5NF

All rights reserved. No part of this publication may be reproduced, stored in
a retrieval system, or transmitted, in any form or by any means, electronic,
mechanical, photocopying, recording or otherwise, without the prior permission
of the Copyright owner.

ISBN 0 85066 043 2 (hardback)

ISBN 0 85066 042 4 (paperback)

Distributed in the United States of America and its territories by
Barnes & Noble Inc, 105 Fifth Avenue, New York, New York 10003

CONTENTS

v

PREFACE

TRADITIONALLY demographers have been concerned with the structure of populations as measured by their distribution in broad biological, social and geographical groups and the dynamics of the changes in these groups over time. It is only in recent years that much work has been done on the relations between the aggregate measurements and the biological factors which determine them and also in the biological consequences of population characteristics and movements. Such studies have taken many forms both in the nature of the subjects investigated and the methods used. They range, for example, from mathematical models of regularities in mortality patterns to the tracing of the spread of disease by ancient burials and from computer simulation of the family sizes of women that follow from reproductive probabilities to the ecological consequences of rapid population growth.

Because of these developments, the Society for the Study of Human Biology organised two Symposia at which some of these topics were discussed. The first was held in November, 1967 with the title "Biological Aspects of Demography"; the second in November, 1968 was on "Climatic Challenge and Population Pressure". The interest in the proceedings of the Symposia suggested that there was scope for the publication of a volume of papers. Most of the papers collected here are based on contributions to the first Symposium although some have been rewritten and greatly extended and others brought up to date. One paper is taken from the second Symposium and another has been specially contributed.

Research in biology and in population interact in so many ways with varying degrees of intensity that a tidy categorization is not possible. One consequence is that any brief description such as the title of this volume can only be a broad indication of the contents, which are a sampling and a taste of the diversity of paths along which progress is being made rather than an overview of a territory.

W. BRASS

POPULATION STRUCTURE AND MOVEMENT PATTERNS

A. J. BOYCE*, C. F. KÜCHEMANN and G. A. HARRISON

Anthropology Laboratory, Department of Human Anatomy, University of Oxford

THERE are problems in recognizing and defining Mendelian units in human distribution. The concept of a Mendelian population, normally defined as a group of individuals sharing, at some degree, in a common gene pool, is based on the fact that all individuals are to varying degree related to one another, that is they share at some level of descent one or more common ancestors. Mendelian populations may be considered as a hierarchy of groups at different levels whose rank depends upon changing degrees of relationship. In theory, individuals can be arranged into clusters and these in turn into larger clusters by establishing a matrix of relationships between individuals and clustering on the basis of these relationships. Such units, however, may not correspond to any observed groupings of people which are normally determined by geographical, religious, social and other non-genetic factors. The type of problem with which one is normally confronted is to be presented with some particular grouping and then to have to identify the ideal Mendelian hierarchy within and between units in this grouping.

Many factors determine mating patterns in man and either facilitate or restrict mating between individuals. Typically, because of the limitations it imposes on movement, distance is a fundamental factor determining mate selection. It may therefore be expected that geographical groupings of people, for instance, grouping into villages or towns, will approximate abstract Mendelian units. Religious or social stratification may, of course, be more important

* Present address: Department of Biological Sciences, University of Surrey.

A

when one is considering a single geographical unit but invariably even these factors will form distinct components when matings between spatially separated groups are considered. It follows that the analysis of movement patterns is of critical importance in understanding the organization of human societies into genetic units because it is through movement that genes are exchanged between populations and movement is thus a prime determinant of the geographical pattern of relatedness.

Usually, it is possible to examine only the present-day movement situation but occasionally information about the historical development of movement patterns can be obtained. When this is so, it is possible to consider the effects on genetic structure of changing movement patterns. In this contribution we should like to discuss some of the problems that have emerged from our analysis of parish register and census material in so far as these problems are concerned with general patterns of human movement. Parish register material varies greatly in different parts of the country both in its completeness and in the time span it covers, but from well-preserved registers it is possible to reconstruct a number of parameters of movement, especially those relating to movement due to marriage. Census data, on the other hand, can reveal patterns of overall movement. Censuses of the population of England and Wales have been taken every ten years since 1801 but detailed information on birth-places was not included until 1851. Since the returns for 1871 onwards are not yet available for study the only census data which can be analysed for overall movement patterns are those from the censuses of 1851 and 1861. These census returns are, however, extremely useful, both because of their reliability and because with them it is possible to cover more easily a wider geographical area than with parish register information.

An important parameter bearing on the correspondence between geographical and genetic units is the amount of spatial exogamy (marriage between people from different demographic clusters). Exogamy determines the level of relatedness within and between such clusters. The higher the levels of exogamy the lower the average degree of relatedness within a cluster and the higher the degree between clusters sharing exogamous partners. It can be measured for any particular geographical population, such as an ecclesiastical parish, by comparing the number of marriages involving a partner from outside the population with the total number of marriages

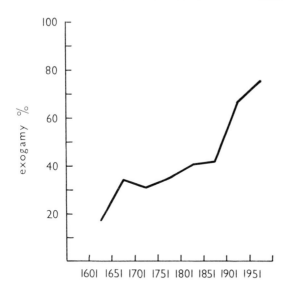

FIG. 1. Changing pattern of exogamy in 50-year periods. Average values
for eight Otmoor parishes.

contracted by members of the population. Analysis of exogamy
rates among Oxfordshire parishes reveals that there has been a
gradual rise in the amount of exogamy over the period for which
information is available, from about 1600 to the present day (see
Fig. 1) and similar trends have been found in other studies of rural
societies (for example, Cavalli-Sforza, 1959). It is of interest to note,
however, that whilst there has been a considerable increase in
exogamy rates, nevertheless even in the earliest period the exogamy
rate was frequently quite high; for instance, among the Oxfordshire
villages we have examined, rates of up to 37 per cent were found in
the period 1601–1650. With such levels of exogamy any tendency
for genetic diversification to occur among the villages must have
been very much less than would appear solely from a cross-sectional
study of the effective population sizes.

The distances over which genes are flowing also influence levels and
patterns of relatedness and effect the likelihood of geographical
genetic variation. So far as gene flow due to marriage is concerned
this movement may be analysed through the examination of distributions of marriage distances. It is possible to consider the distances

A 2

over which marriages are contracted between the members of a village and other villages in two ways. The first consists of the examination of the relationship between frequency of marriage with the members of a particular village and the distance of that village from the one being considered. Analysis of the data from one of the Oxfordshire villages, Charlton-on-Otmoor, has shown that the frequency of marriage with members of a particular village decreases non-linearly with increasing distance and this pattern has been interpreted in terms of a model of neighbourhood knowledge (Boyce *et al.*, 1967). Marriage distances can also be examined in terms of the total contribution of marriage partners that are made to any one village by all villages at a given distance from it and from a distribution constructed in this way a mean marriage distance can be calculated. Such a distribution of marriage distances is highly J-shaped (Fig. 2) although there is evidence that over very short distances (e.g. up to 6 miles) there is little or no decrease in frequency of contributions with increasing distance. In other words, over such

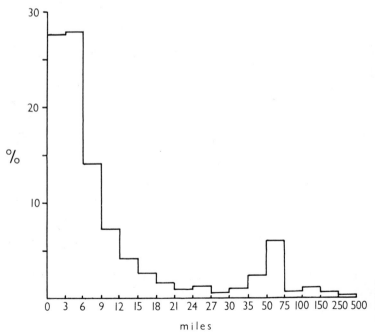

miles

FIG. 2. Distribution of exogamous marriage distances.

short distances the decline in individual village contributions is more or less exactly balanced by the increasing number of villages.

The fact that the overall distribution of marriage distances is highly skewed raises the problem of the relationship between distance and degree of relatedness. It is necessary, at this point, to distinguish between relationship in the genealogical sense and relationship in terms of degree of genetic similarity. Commonly, estimates of closeness of relationship are based upon the degree of genetic similarity established for as many genetic systems as possible and those populations with the most similar gene pools are said to be the most closely related, however the similarity may have arisen. On the other hand, for defining the genetic structure of populations it is most meaningful to consider relationship in the genealogical sense irrespective of genetic similarity. If there is genetic heterogeneity among populations then, in the absence of convergence and differential rates of diversification, the two estimates of relatedness will be very similar but it is of course possible to have varying degrees of genealogical relationship within and between population units which are genetically homogeneous.

One would expect the degree of genealogical relationship between population units to be related to their distance apart in a manner closely determined by the shape of the marriage distribution. The actual calculation of degree of relationship between populations is, however, a difficult problem since it also depends upon such factors as relative sizes of the populations and the cumulative effect of gene flow over successive generations. A further complication is introduced by the fact that the average distance over which genes are flowing changes with time. This is shown very clearly when mean marriage distance is plotted over a long period of time. For example, in Fig. 3, in which mean marriage distance for the villages of the Otmoor area is plotted for a 360-year period, it is clear that there was a dramatic increase in mean marriage distance with the arrival of mechanized forms of transport in the middle of the 19th century, which obviously increased the area over which genes were flowing in any particular generation. It is nevertheless interesting that the change in mean marriage distance which occurred at that time appears from an analysis of the distribution of marriage distances before and after the period of change to be due to a superimposition of a new phenomenon (the choice of marriage partners from places at relatively great distances away) onto a basic pattern of selection

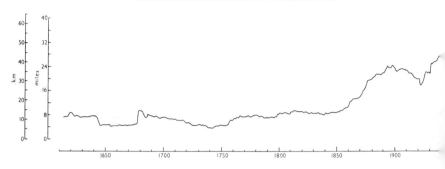

FIG. 3. Mean marriage distance in the Otmoor area plotted as a 25-year moving average

of partners from places within the immediate locality, a pattern which has remained virtually unchanged throughout the period studied.

When considering degree of exogamy and the distribution of marriage distances, movement was assumed to take place freely in all directions but observation of actual movement patterns shows this to be a false assumption and that the pattern is frequently asymmetric. This asymmetry has two components, one is the general orientation of movement, that is, axes along which most movement occurs, and the second is the direction of movement along these axes. Insight into the general orientation of movement can be obtained by plotting on a geographical basis the relative contributions of marriage partners made to one population unit by the units in its vicinity. A series of contours, lines of constant contribution, can be drawn through these relative contributions. The symmetry of these contours and the way in which they are arranged with respect to one another provide information about the orientation of move-ment. For example, Fig. 4 shows an actual contour map for the village of Charlton in which the relative contributions of neigh-bouring villages to the total number of exogamous marriages over the 360-year period involving Charlton are shown. Contours at fixed intervals have been plotted and show that even in a village which is central to an open and fairly homogeneous agricultural area there is a distinct orientation to the marriage movement. In particular, one can detect a clear NE/SW trend and it is evident that this is partly due to variations in the sizes of villages. For instance, in the north-east there is the comparatively large town of Bicester

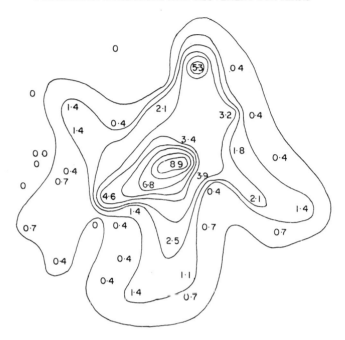

FIG. 4. Contributions (per cent) to Charlton exogamous marriages of villages within 6 miles of Charlton.

which has made a large contribution to the breeding population of Charlton over the 360-year period. It is possible to minimize the effects of variations in population size when setting up the contour maps and if this is done the effects of local geography are shown to play a part in determining the orientation of movement—in particular the presence of the swampy, somewhat impassable area of the Ot Moor and the pattern of roadways in the area. (Although there has no doubt been considerable feedback between the orientation of movement and the development of the road pattern.)

The use of the contour model helps in understanding the distribution of marriage distances. A section along a radius of the contour map should, in the symmetrical situation, correspond to the curve relating frequency of marriage between members of the central village and of another village to the distance of the second village from the focal one. Where there is asymmetry due to orientation of movement this latter curve is only an approximation and can be interpreted meaningfully only if frequent consideration is given to the actual geographical pattern of movement. A plot of the distances of villages falling between successive contours of fixed contribution bears a direct relationship to the overall distribution of marriage distances and the contour map is thus also a map of the pattern of relatedness.

In theory, directional orientation of movement could be detected by measuring the reciprocal movement between different population units. Some insight into reciprocal movement can be obtained from both parish register and census material although parish register material must be extensively linked before this information can be obtained. Similarly, unless census data is analysed over a very wide area it is difficult to obtain information on absolute amounts of exchange since the census returns for any particular place indicate where people come from but not where they go to. However, the relative degree of interchange between pairs of villages will give a clue to the direction of movement since in the absence of directional movement one would expect the extents to which villages give to and receive from each other to be equal. If, on the other hand, there is a geographical trend to this ratio, then it will represent the overall direction of movement. Using census data solely as a guide to marriage movement, i.e. considering only those husband–wife pairs where one partner was born in the village of residence and the other elsewhere, the Oxfordshire study has shown there to be little directional tendency to marriage movement. However, the overall giving/ receiving ratio for villages in the Otmoor area shows a geographical pattern with villages in the NE having ratios greater than 1 and villages in the SW ratios of less than 1. It may therefore be concluded that there is an overall direction towards the SW in the movement pattern.

The four components of movement which have been considered here, the degree of exogamy, the distribution of marriage distances, the orientation and the direction of movement are of critical importance not only in determining the pattern of relatedness in human populations but also in considering many other aspects of genetic structure. Although the study we have described is only in its initial stages we hope that this discussion has indicated the wide and general importarce of the analysis of human movement patterns.

Acknowledgement

Grateful acknowledgement is made to the Nuffield Foundation for a grant in support of this research.

References

BOYCE, A. J., KÜCHEMANN, C. H. and HARRISON, G. A. (1967) Neighbourhood knowledge and the distribution of marriage distances, *Ann. hum. Genet. Lond.* **30**, 335–338.

CAVALLI-SFORZA, L. L. (1959) Some data on the genetics of human populations, *Proc. X Int. Congress of Genetics* **1**, 389–407.

A MONTE CARLO SIMULATION OF REPRODUCTION

J. C. BARRETT

London School of Hygiene & Tropical Medicine, University of London

I SHALL describe, chiefly from a mathematical point of view, some preliminary work on a model of the changes produced in a population as a result of events connected with human reproduction, together with a computer simulation of the model. A simulation proceeds in a different direction and spirit from a statistical analysis. It is generally a synthesis of a system from information (or assumptions) about the components, for example the production of demographic change from the behaviour of individuals. The present simulation is by a Monte Carlo method; that is, by subjecting random numbers to numerical processes. The random numbers are used to establish the timing or outcome of events by means of probabilities, such as the probability that a woman will conceive in a given month, and the probability that the result of conception will be a live birth. It is not necessary to suppose that elements of unpredictability are really attached always to such events, but it is convenient to represent the relative frequencies in this way. By this means, information about the factors associated with natality can be built directly into the model, and the micro-structure of the population can be studied. The effect of biological factors, such as different distributions of sterility and various incidences of foetal death and stillbirth, on birth spacing and on fertility rates is simulated. (The word "fertility" is used here in the demographic sense of the actual level of births, as distinct from fecundity, the potential level.) Such simulations provide not only results that can be calculated by other methods, for example the mean delay per birth interval caused by pregnancy wastage (Westoff *et al.*, 1961), but also quantities such

11

as distributions of family sizes, on which the effect of changing sterility, etc. is difficult to calculate in any other way.

The Monte Carlo method has been used in different forms and situations for many decades, but it obtained its chief impetus in the second world war, from problems of neutron diffusion. Kahn (1962), who developed it extensively, has described it as the estimation of the expected score by averaging the results of a large number of plays of a game of chance. The original problem need not refer to probabilities provided that it can be made equivalent for some purposes to the calculation of an expected score; but the method is, I think, often more successful when the difficulty or impossibility of predicting events makes the problem inherently stochastic, involving random variables. Nor is access to a computer in principle essential to the method. De Bethune (1963) has described a procedure which is, I think, essentially a Monte Carlo simulation, effected by drawing coloured marbles at random to determine child spacing, in a series of simulated statistical experiments. But the availability of digital computers with greater speeds and store sizes makes the use of the method increasingly feasible. The representation of individual events gives more power than analytic methods to deal with such complexities as changing probabilities, non-linearities and special cases, and can provide the *raison d'être* of Monte Carlo simulation in problems whose solution is not feasible by comparatively precise methods of analysis.

The most extensive simulations of human reproduction and fertility have been those of Sheps and her associates in America (Sheps and Ridley, 1965; Ridley and Sheps, 1966; Sheps and Perrin, 1966), and of Hyrenius and others in Sweden (Hyrenius and Adolfsson, 1964; Hyrenius et al., 1966; Hyrenius, 1965). The formulation of a model involves the definition of assumptions and hypotheses, which can be useful in itself. But as Ridley, Sheps and others have shown, such models allow not only more precise descriptions but also a form of experimentation. Controlled experiments in which factors can be varied separately are difficult to organize and not often possible or desirable in demography, and it is often difficult to distinguish the effects of different factors in the data obtained from censuses and surveys. By simulation, however, the relevant parameters may be changed individually and their importance assessed, since the conditions in which the data are generated are known. On the other hand, the artificiality of models must be constantly borne in mind; and their validation and comparison, like that of other scientific hypotheses, raise general questions about scientific method.

The influence of preferred sizes of families, although a very important aspect of contemporary demography, is not considered at this stage in the present model. Instead, the model deals with populations in which no attempt is made to influence family size, and no dissolutions of marriage, for example by widowhood, occur. Modifications to allow for circumstances such as these may be introduced at a later date, by means of tables of nuptiality, divorce and mortality rates, or perhaps by a subsidiary program in which effective marriage durations are computed. Apart from these restrictions, the model is a general one, and in order to set it up it has been necessary to make use of a variety of sources and population data. As the model develops, they may be replaced by more homogeneous data.

The development of the model has been influenced by some related work in non-human populations. An example of the use of the Monte Carlo method in an area, cell population kinetics, that is in a number of ways analogous to the present one, is a Monte Carlo simulation of the mitotic cycle (Barrett, 1966a, b) in which random numbers were used to represent durations of phases associated with the synthesis of deoxyribose nucleic acid in individual mammalian cells, allowing cell generation times, cell age distributions and cell population doubling times to be compared with the values measured by biophysical methods, and to be related to the growth of a tumour. In another tumour a substantial extent of cell loss or migration was indicated by this means. The fact of transmission of information between cells, both genetically and through their environment, and the effect on cell proliferation, may in future, I think, make the analogy between these two fields more than a mathematical connexion, and perhaps useful in the cytological aspects of cancer research, ageing and the recovery of tissues from injury, as well as in the demography of population growth, of population ageing, and of migration. See Espinas (1877) and Fürth (1952) for a discussion of related questions.

Many workers have constructed mathematical models of the life cycles of animals, and life tables for animal populations are available also. For example, Deevey (1947) has described a variety of life tables ranging, when plotted logarithmically, from a concave type considered typical of mackerel and oysters to a convex type for mountain sheep and other mammals, with those of birds approximately to the intermediate case of constant age-specific mortality. Dean and Galloway (1965) used a computer program that takes account of varying sex ratios, breeding periods and harem sizes, etc. in the reproduction cycle of animals. Mathematical models applied to the reproductive cycle of man himself are apposite, not only because of man's particular interest and special significance, but also because of the amount of data available for use with such models. As Newcombe (1965) has pointed out in describing the large amount of information about people that is gathered routinely for a variety of purposes in modern societies, "For no organism other than man have the facts of procreation and family composition, and of mortality and morbidity, been so minutely documented over such large populations." Moreover, as Professor Barnicot (1958) said at a symposium held by this society, "There are wide areas of physical anthropology in which work on animals can be no adequate substitute for information about man himself, and it is therefore worthwhile . . . devising techniques by which it can be obtained."

In the present model the reproductive history of a cohort of women is simulated from the beginning of marriage to the end of the reproductive span of life. Cohort methods have certain advantages in demography, arising partly from a tendency for quantities such as family sizes to become more stable as they reach completion, a negative feedback process that tends to diminish the demographic effects of perturbations resulting from wars and economic depressions. Be that as it may, a cohort method is adopted in the present work because it appears to be the most natural procedure for a microanalytic simulation. The time variables are regarded as discrete, and events occur only at intervals of one (lunar) month, with 13 months to a year, a definition that applies here whenever "month" refers to the simulation. From the start of marriage, there is the possibility of conception, with probability p per month. The result of conception is either a foetal death, a stillbirth or a live birth. A live birth is defined here as a confinement at which one or more children are born alive. The fecundability p denotes the probability that a woman will conceive in any month, not the probability of a conception leading only to a live birth, which some workers call the "effective fecundability" (Sheps and Perrin, 1964).

The history of each woman is simulated in turn, from the start of

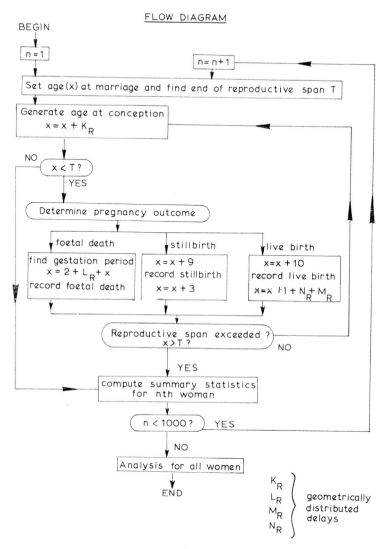

FLOW DIAGRAM

marriage at, say, $T_0 = 20$ years, until the end T_m of the reproductive span, through a series of states, the first of which is susceptibility to conception. For this state, random numbers distributed between 0 and 1 are generated successively (one for each month) until a random number less than ρ is obtained. In this way a geometric distribution of time to conception is simulated, with mean $(1-\rho)/\rho$

months and variance $(1 - \rho)/\rho^2$ months^2. For example, a fecundability of 0·2 per month is equivalent to a mean time to conception of 4 months. With this method there is no difficulty in modifying the fecundability ρ to become a function of time or age (Hyrenius and Adolfsson, 1964), or of parity; but it is treated as independent of these quantities at present, and it is considered that this may be realistic for a large part of the reproductive span. Information regarding the variation of fecundability with time has been provided by the work of Henry (1958, 1965) on the fertility of couples in Normandy married between 1674 and 1742. He attributed increases in intervals between successive confinements chiefly to an increasing delay in the resumption of ovulation after a confinement. He also considered that large families were more often associated with shorter intervals of insusceptibility following a live birth than with higher levels of fecundability. Potter *et al.* (1965) also found that in Punjabi women the increase in birth spacing among older women was due to factors other than reduced fecundability. On the other hand, differences in fecundability between women (Brass, 1958; Dandekar, 1963) are considered sufficiently important to warrant inclusion in the model.

A further random number is used to determine the outcome of conception, according to the probabilities θ_2, θ_3, θ_4 assigned to foetal death, stillbirth and live birth. The duration of pregnancy is represented by fixed times for stillbirth and live births (9 and 10 lunar months respectively), and by random numbers from a geometric distribution for foetal deaths. An interval of insusceptibility to conception follows the end of pregnancy. This interval of insusceptibility is regarded as constant for foetal deaths and still-births, and unimodally distributed following a live birth. After the insusceptible interval the woman returns to the first state and conceives again, unless the end of the reproductive span is reached first. Several types of distribution have been used for the duration of the interval of post-partum insusceptibility following a live birth. A triangular distribution was used at first, similar to the distribution described by Hyrenius and Adolfsson (1964). This was changed later to a fixed delay followed by two geometrically distributed delays, the combination of which allows the findings of Potter *et al.* (1965) and of Dandekar (1959) to be taken into account.

In most cases the fixed component has been one (lunar) month, and the parameters for the variable components for the simulated distributions have been one-sixth per month. This corresponds to a mean delay of 11 months and a standard deviation of 7·75 months. Potter and his co-workers found that the mean duration of the insusceptible interval in Punjabi women was 10·8 (calendar) months with a standard deviation of 7·4 months. It seems likely that this population was not entirely non-contracepting, but this should not affect the estimates appreciably. On the other hand, the values may be increased as a result of prolonged breast-feeding, to which Potter *et al.* (1965) attributes the difference between the mean birth intervals for Punjabi women and for Western populations such as the Hutterite sect in America (31 months compared to 26 months). The Hutterites are a very fertile, religious sect who are presumed to do nothing to restrict family size. The importance of the post-partum insusceptible interval was shown in the simulation of Ridley and Sheps (1966), who were able to obtain a closer correspondence to Indian natality levels by allowing for the prolongation of this interval in lactating women, although the real extent of this prolongation still seems uncertain. Nutritional factors also contribute to the shorter duration of the interval in American, compared to Indian, women (Salber, Feinleib and MacMahon, 1966). In addition to the factors mentioned, infant mortality also has a direct effect on birth intervals, at least in some countries.

For the gestation interval preceding a foetal death a triangular distribution was again used initially, in line with previous work (Shapiro *et al.*, 1962; Hyrenius *et al.*, 1966); but it was subsequently changed to a geometric distribution, which is closer to the extensive data of French and Bierman (1962) for foetal mortality on the island of Kauai. The extent of spontaneous foetal mortality is not always recognized. These workers found that about 24 per cent of conceptions end in foetal death (in which term I shall include embryonic death), decreasing from a maximum of 108 losses per 1000 women under observation for the 4–7 week period. The monotonic decreasing curve of French and Bierman is in accordance with the statement of Erhardt (1952) that "there is a group of unknown size which is unlikely ever to be reported, namely, those which are unrecognized as termination of an early pregnancy, and those which terminate without requiring or receiving medical attention". In fact, it is likely that even greater losses occur in the first month of gestation, in view of the observations of Hertig *et al.* (1959) for women treated for therapeutic hysterectomy. It may be pertinent to mention that a

B

similar high rate of loss early in gestation is found in other mammals (Brambell, 1948). In Rhesus monkeys (Heuser and Streeter, 1941), workers at the Carnegie Embryological Laboratory found a pre-natal mortality rate of well over 30 per cent of all fertilized ova; and in foxes, pre-natal mortalities of about 30 per cent are found (Layne, 1958). The present computer program causes the probability of foetal death to decrease from 0·11 in the second month of gestation to $P_n = P_{n-1} \times 0·55$ in the nth month ($3 \leqslant n \leqslant 8$), losses in the first month being regarded as equivalent to reduced fecundability.

Sterility is introduced into the model as a linear function of the woman's age, after a fixed age. Like fecundability, it depends in reality, of course, on both parties to the marriage, but for simplicity is attributed entirely to the woman in this model. Secondary sterility, on the other hand, and its possible dependence on parity, is not yet included. Tabular data representing the distribution of ages at menopause are part of the input to the program. The table of data in use at present represents the Pearson Type I distribution of Hyrenius *et al.* (1966), with mean 47·6 years and mode 48·7 years. In the program, one random number (z) is generated at the beginning of the simulation of each woman's history to determine directly the age at which sterility would occur ($y_1 = z/s_1 + 20$), and a second random number is used to determine the age z_1 at menopause. The lesser of these two ages y_1, z_1 is taken as the end T_m of the re-productive span for the particular woman. After every conception and pregnancy her age is tested in the program to establish whether the end of the reproductive span has been reached. If it has, the program causes summary statistics to be computed, and proceeds with the next woman's history.

The probabilities θ_2, θ_3, θ_4 of foetal death, stillbirth and live birth can furthermore be made to depend linearly on the woman's age (r years) in program:

$$\theta_2 = C_2 + (r - 30)S_2/10,$$
$$\theta_3 = C_3 + (r - 30)S_3/10,$$
$$\theta_3 = 1 - \theta_2 - \theta_4.$$

Typical values used are $C_2 = 0·24$, $C_3 = 0·03$, $S_1 = 0·01$ per year, $S_2 = 0·05$ per year, $S_3 = 0·01$ per year, as in run 2.

The Monte Carlo program is written in the FORTRAN language and generates a series of pseudo-random numbers by the multiplicative congruential method. The sub-routine RANDOM (Z)

Table A. Specification of runs

	Run number						
	1	2	3	4	5	6	7
e at rriage (yrs)	20	20	20	20	20	30	35
cundability r month)	0·2	0·2	0·2	0·2	0·2	0·2	0·2
nopause	Const.	Var.	As run 2	As run 2	As run 2	As run 2	As run 2
rility	0	$0·01(t-20)$	0	As run 2	0	As run 2	As run 2
etal deaths	0·24	$0·24+0·05(t-30)$	0·24	0·24	As run 2	As run 2	As run 2
lbirths	0·02	$0·03+0·01(t-30)$	0·03	0·03	As run 2	As run 2	As run 2

that generates uniformly distributed random numbers in this way may be called upon either by the main programme, or, when a geometric distribution is required for any of the purposes mentioned earlier (time to conception, etc.), by a second sub-routine that continues to call for random numbers z until one is obtained in a required range $(0, R)$. For later cases involving low fecundabilities (R), a more efficient method of obtaining geometrically distributed random numbers by means of $((\log z)/\log(1-R))-0·5$ was substituted.

The results obtained from several runs of the computer program, each for 1000 women, will be described next. The second run is considered more realistic than the first, although the input parameters for it differ in only four respects from those of the first, namely, in the simulation of variable age at menopause, and in the linear increases in sterility and in probabilities of foetal death and stillbirth with the age of the mother. For the first run the probability of sterility, foetal death, stillbirth and live birth was taken as independent of the woman's age, and their respective values were set to 0, 0·24, 0·02 and 0·74. The age at the end of the reproductive span of life was uniformly distributed between 40 and 41 years; while for the second run the age at menopause varied between 38 and 53 years according to a Pearson Type I distribution as described earlier, giving a mean age of 43·8 years at the end of the reproductive span in the second run, after allowing for the effect of variable sterility.

The remaining input parameters for both runs were as follows: Fecundability was 0·2 per (lunar) month. Age at marriage was 20 years (260 months). A foetal death was followed by a fixed delay of 2 months. A live birth at 10 months was followed by a fixed delay of 1 month and two successive geometrically distributed delays with paramaters 0·1667 per month. A stillbirth at 9 months was followed by a fixed delay of 3 months before the interval of susceptibility to further conception.

TABLE 1 (run 1). Age of nth woman at $j-1$th birth (lunar months)

	$j=1$	2	3	4	5	6	7	8	9	10	11	12	13
$n=1$	260	274	288	313	340	383	399	419	440	471	495	529	0
2	260	274	293	314	347	382	405	428	468	492	518	0	0
3	260	299	335	358	381	409	447	469	506	517	534	0	0
4	260	270	298	342	375	393	407	434	472	494	520	0	0
5	260	279	295	341	357	389	413	445	471	487	509	527	0

TABLE 2 (run 2). Age of nth woman at $j-1$th birth (lunar months)

	$j=1$	2	3	4	5	6	7	8	9	10	11	12	13	14	15
$n=1$	260	278	303	0	0	0	0	0	0	0	0	0	0	0	0
2	260	287	306	334	369	416	441	478	526	543	570	583	630	644	0
3	260	292	328	351	386	414	431	500	517	545	0	0	0	0	0
4	260	274	307	367	426	461	478	504	534	565	583	0	0	0	0
5	260	277	305	333	358	379	398	449	465	482	527	582	601	0	0

The ages of the women (in months) are computed for each birth, but only the values for the first few women are printed out by the computer. These are shown in Tables 1 and 2 as an illustration of the sort of random variation that occurs. In Table 2 it can be seen that the first woman in run 2 became sterile some time after the second live birth. In Table 1 the long time to the first live birth of the third woman (39 months) almost certainly indicates that one or more foetal deaths or stillbirths supervened. Complete reproductive sequences of this kind have an important bearing on techniques for the appraisal of population control measures, since the sequences can provide information about the extent to which chance effects produce high fertility in a few women at an early age, even without any variation in fecundability between women, and this phenomenon should be taken into account before any subsequent reduction in the fertility of these particular women is attributed to new factors.

Run 3 is identical to run 2 except that sterility is omitted and that the probabilities of foetal death (0·24), of stillbirth (0·03) and live birth (0·73) are independent of each woman's age. Runs 4 and 5 are identical to run 2 except that sterility is omitted in run 5, and foetal death and stillbirth probabilities are constant in run 4. The distribution of foetal deaths, stillbirths and live births for these runs are shown in Tables 3, 4 and 5.

In natural data a negative skewness of the distribution of live births is found in populations in which little or no attempt is made to restrict family size. Thus data for the Census of Ireland (1911),

TABLE 3. Numbers of women with n foetal deaths

	Run number						
n	1	2	3	4	5	6	7
0	41	75	15	73	15	209	263
1	123	127	80	115	61	132	189
2	266	92	131	167	101	181	191
3	199	187	176	172	144	139	159
4	166	148	169	151	163	121	101
5	98	116	180	115	159	97	59
6	52	121	96	101	141	54	24
7	43	65	82	52	93	36	10
8	12	49	31	25	56	14	2
9	0	13	21	20	33	9	2
10	0	7	9	6	20	4	0
11	0	0	7	0	7	3	0
12	0	0	3	2	4	1	0
13	0	0	0	1	0	0	0
14	0	0	0	0	3	0	0
15	0	0	0	0	0	0	0
Total	1000	1000	1000	1000	1000	1000	1000

TABLE 4. Numbers of women with n stillbirths

n	Run number						
	1	2	3	4	5	6	7
0	740	612	602	648	561	703	757
1	246	275	312	291	328	228	205
2	7	99	71	54	89	61	29
3	6	7	11	7	17	8	8
4	1	7	4	0	3	0	1
5	0	0	0	0	2	0	0
6	0	0	0	0	0	0	0
Total	1000	1000	1000	1000	1000	1000	1000

TABLE 5. Number of women with n live births

n	Run number						
	1	2	3	4	5	6	7
0	0	0	0	6	0	114	147
1	0	26	0	29	0	22	22
2	0	15	0	27	0	19	35
3	0	19	0	21	0	28	92
4	0	42	0	26	0	46	137
5	0	28	0	18	0	75	179
6	0	27	0	21	0	101	164
7	14	34	2	26	3	133	112
8	137	34	15	27	10	142	72
9	346	42	37	48	42	161	34
10	254	117	73	93	115	98	6
11	168	120	145	118	139	44	0
12	69	159	167	152	169	15	0
13	12	161	194	114	199	2	0
14	0	82	169	129	149	0	0
15	0	59	103	90	95	0	0
16	0	21	61	41	46	0	0
17	0	14	30	12	26	0	0
18	0	0	4	1	5	0	0
19	0	0	0	1	2	0	0
20	0	0	0	0	0	0	0
Total	1000	1000	1000	1000	1000	1000	1000

Table 165K, give a skewness with a Pearson coefficient of -0.31 ± 0.08 for the almost completed family size distribution of women who had married at ages between 20 and 25. This fact is rather surprising in view of distributions of fecundability (which theoretically ranges between 0 and 1) that are probably positively skewed. Consequently it is interesting that in the Monte Carlo simulation runs 1 to 5, negative skewness (in runs 2 and 4, Table 5) appears to result from the introduction of sterility into the model, and that the net effect of the other factors introduced so far, including the influence of menopause data, is comparatively small as regards the skewness of the live birth distribution. In this way, simulation can show the extent to which an effect such as the negative skewness of the live birth distribution is cancelled or reinforced when various parameter values or distributions are chosen for the different factors, such as sterility.

There are two further phenomena revealed in preliminary simulation runs. The first is the "truncation" effect. The mean time (per live birth, not per woman) between successive live births in run 3 was 28.4 ± 0.2 months. The value calculated according to the theoretical analysis by renewal theory of Perrin and Sheps (1964) is 28.7 months. The present simulation of test cases has usually given values for the mean time between successive live births about 0.3 months less than calculated, and in the process of resolving the difference, a "truncation" effect was revealed, which has been independently found by Sheps et al. (1967). This effect results from the fact that the reproductive span of life of a woman is terminated at a finite age; so conceptions that occur just before that age are counted, while those that would have occurred just after are not, with a consequent reduction in the mean and variance of the birth intervals. Another way (Sheps et al., 1967) of looking at the effect is that only a woman who happens to have relatively short intervals can have a relatively large number of births; so high order intervals tend to be short. The effect is therefore a real one. It is, however, opposed by a natural tendency for later birth intervals to increase, as a result, for example, of increases with age in the probabilities of foetal deaths and stillbirths; so in runs 2 and 5, when these features were incorporated in the simulation as linear functions of age, no reduction in the overall mean time between live births was found (Table 8). Subsequent runs have shown that although the truncation effect on the overall mean time between live births is small, the effect on the high order intervals is quite pronounced. The effect should therefore be allowed for in any assessment of successive changes in birth intervals from demographic data, especially if inferences about age dependency are to be made.

TABLE 6. Live births and foetal deaths

Distribution to mothers	Total	Foetal deaths	Rate per 1000
7 and under	468	118	252
8–10	478	104	218
11–12	794	145	183
13	884	162	183
14	1148	260	226
15	1365	316	232
16	1648	363	220
17	1734	407	235
18	1836	463	252
19	1425	375	263
20	1120	323	288
21	651	236	363
22+	923	319	346
	14,474	3,591	248

The second phenomenon is associated with stillbirths and foetal deaths. In run 4 and subsequent runs, the numbers of live births were cross classified by numbers of foetal deaths and by numbers of stillbirths. The distribution of live births and foetal deaths combined is shown in Table 6 for run 4, together with the proportions resulting in foetal deaths. It might appear from this table that an increased number of pregnancies per woman results in an increased foetal death ratio; but in fact the probability of foetal death is constant for this run, being the same for all women and independent of their ages. The explanation of this phenomenon, which has some importance for the interpretation of vital statistics, is that a foetal death decreases the period of exposure to risk of conception less than a live birth does; so it is the occurrence of a high foetal death ratio that results in a large number of pregnancies, rather than vice versa. At the other end of the scale the foetal death ratio is also high, since it approaches, for women who had only one pregnancy, the probability of foetal death when stillbirths are ignored. Thus, although the probabilities of conception, foetal death, etc. are constant for this run, the foetal death ratio has the concave shape of distribution that actually occurs in practice. In Table 7 similar data are given for stillbirths; the effect is smaller since stillbirths are fewer and produce less reduction overall in the period of risk. Live births were classified by women's ages for runs 4 and 5 (Table 8), but since each run represents only 1000 women, there are appreciable sampling effects.

TABLE 7. Live births and stillbirths

Distribution to mothers	Total	Stillbirths	Rate per 1000
6 and under	460	18	39
7–9	618	20	32
10	820	27	33
11	1067	38	36
12	1680	57	34
13	1664	76	46
14	1960	61	31
15	1530	50	33
16	912	34	37
17+	592	39	66
	11,303	420	37

Two further runs were carried out in order to investigate the effect of delaying the age at marriage from 20 years in run 2 to 30 years in run 6 and 35 years in run 7, with the same initial conditions (i.e. sterility assumed to increase from age 20 onwards, etc.). In runs 6 and 7 the mean number of live births is reduced, and the proportions of women having no live births is increased (Table 5). This result is to be expected, and can be seen, for example, in the data of the Census of Ireland (1911), Tables 165K and 166K, for marriages of completed fertility and various ages at marriage, although the mean family sizes are smaller there. On the other hand, the proportion of women having 1 or 2 live births, for the later ages at marriage in runs 6 and 7, remains much the same as in run 2, in contrast to the data for Ireland.

TABLE 8. Further live birth statistics

Age	Live births per 1000 women	
	Run 4	Run 5
20–	2119	2275
25–	2069	2304
30–	2022	2245
35–	1866	2203
40–	1637	2030
45–	980	1283
50–	190	250
55–60	0	0

	Run			
	2	3	4	5
Mean time between live births (lunar months)	28·6	28·4	28·3	28·7
Variance (months²)	141	132	131	147
Total live births	10,569	12,787	10,883	12,590

Such differences between real and simulated distributions suggest refinements in the assumptions and the accuracy of the model, e.g. as regards variations in fecundability, and non-linear age changes in sterility. Accordingly, a uniform distribution of fecundability between women, and a parameter K representing the age (previously 20 years) at which sterility begins to increase, were introduced into the model. The fecundability of each woman is then determined at the beginning of each run by a random number drawn from a uniform distribution with mean ρ and specified width. Results (Table 9) similar to the data for Ireland (Table 10) were obtained when sterility was taken as 4·8 per cent until age $K=28$ years, increasing linearly at 1·18 per cent per year thereafter, and fecundability was uniformly distributed between 0 and 0·21. The other parameters were as in run 2. The sizes of samples of women married

TABLE 9. Numbers of women with n live births

| | Age at marriage (years) | | | | | |
n	19·0	22·5	27·5	32·5	37·5	42·5
0	24	68	57	82	55	29
1	0	3	33	21	25	21
2	1	18	39	37	58	28
3	8	51	52	60	65	23
4	15	67	78	99	62	24
5	19	73	110	99	40	5
6	24	119	161	87	17	1
7	44	157	143	58	7	—
8	44	202	156	47	2	—
9	71	203	107	19	1	—
10	70	177	67	5	—	—
11	56	127	21	1	—	—
12	55	80	9	—	—	—
13	36	30	4	—	—	—
14	13	14	1	—	—	—
15	11	6	—	—	—	·
16	5	1	—	—	—	—
17	—	—	—	—	—	—
Total	496	1396	1038	615	332	131

at each age were chosen as 10 per cent of the corresponding Census totals. The two sterility parameters were obtained from the incidence of childlessness in Table 10, and the two fecundability parameters were varied until satisfactory agreement was obtained between the graphs of cumulative distributions of children of women married at ages between 20 and 25 years and of simulated live births for women married at 22·5 years. For the latter the mean time between simulated live births was 35·2 (lunar) months. (In this case, in which the range of fecundability extends to zero, the mean live birth interval remains finite because the reproductive span of life is of finite extent.)

Using the same parameters for marriages at ages over 25, the fecundability then appears to be underestimated. There are several possible explanations for this discrepancy, apart from shortcomings in the model for simulation. Since the women in all the age groups shown in Table 165K married in approximately the same years (1876–1881), the oldest groups represent earlier birth cohorts. These

TABLE 10. (Table 165K, Census of Ireland, 1911). Numbers of families in which n children were born alive, for marriages of 30 and under 35 years' duration

			Age of wife at marriage				
n	Under 20	20–25	25–30	30–35	35–40	40–45	45–50	Total
0	193	654	647	557	510	515	130	3206
1	75	255	230	229	263	193	18	1263
2	79	318	300	284	369	172	18	1540
3	129	431	450	431	411	136	11	1999
4	225	601	744	675	494	93	4	2836
5	224	813	915	865	384	64	4	3269
6	319	1162	1252	881	311	49	—	3974
7	402	1388	1413	740	248	31	—	4222
8	481	1740	1448	567	151	28	—	4415
9	571	1806	1185	371	71	12	—	4016
10	635	1768	823	260	54	14	—	3554
11	553	1255	462	135	29	—	—	2434
12	442	859	259	80	12	—	—	1652
Over 12	636	915	255	70	13	—	—	1889
Total	4964	13,965	10,383	6145	3320	1307	185	40,269

older married women may therefore have been selected for different sociological or demographic characteristics, including fertility; also they may be less likely to have had even a small degree of family limitation at later ages. The older women may also have been more inclined to include on the Census form children born before their current marriage. The existence of some such differences is in fact suggested by a consideration of the amount of childlessness in the other Census tables.

At the same time it is evident that for the principal age groups married between ages 20 and 25, the simulation gives rather too few women with 2 to 5, or more than 12, live births. Subsequent runs have shown that the agreement is not much increased by making the post partum variation different between women, and is decreased by varying the fecundability at each conception instead of only at the beginning of each woman's history. The fact that it is necessary to extend a uniform distribution of fecundability to zero to obtain agreement by means of the present model may suggest that there is little apparent distinction between low fecundability and biological sterility for the marriages in the Census population. These last suggestions will require further investigation, because the effects of other types of distributions for the post partum interval and for fecundability have yet to be simulated, and because there are several types of variation not yet completely incorporated.

Apart from increasing the accuracy of the input parameters and functions, and perhaps relaxing the assumptions about independence, in order to obtain more realism for particular populations, there are several ways in which the model may be developed. For example, it would be possible by means of a loop in the program to trace the histories not only of a cohort of women but also of their female children (whose birth times are produced by the computer program) for a few generations, e.g. until a stable age distribution is almost reached, a procedure that might provide information about the dynamics of population change. By simulating fecundability as a function of parity or age or both, future family sizes may be gauged, or population policies appraised.

Acknowledgement

I should like to acknowledge the guidance I have received from Mr. W. Brass in this work.

References

BARNICOT, N. A. (1958) The experimental approach to physical anthropology, *The Scope of Physical Anthropology and its Place in Academic Studies*, edited by D. F. Roberts and J. S. Wiener, pp. 31–34, The Society for Human Biology, London.

BARRETT, J. C. (1966a) A mathematical model of the mitotic cycle, *J. Natn. Cancer Inst.* **37**, 443–450.

BARRETT, J. C. (1966b) Studies in Cell Proliferation, with particular reference to the use of Monte Carlo simulation in the interpretation of isotopic labelling experiments, Ph.D. Thesis, University of London.

BRAMBELL, F. W. R. (1948) Prenatal mortality in mammals, *Biol. Rev.* **23**, 370–407.

BRASS, W. (1958) The distribution of births in human populations, *Popul. Studies* **12**(1), 51–72.

CENSUS OF IRELAND (1911) *General Report, Tables 165K, 166K*, H.M.S.O., London, 1913.

DANDEKAR, K. (1959) Intervals between confinements, *Eugen. Q.* **6**(3), 180–186.

DANDEKAR, K. (1963) Analysis of birth intervals of a set of Indian women, *Eugen. Q.* **10**(2), 73–78.

DEAN, F. C. and GALLOWAY, G. A. (1965) A Fortran program for population study with minimal computer training, *J. Wildl. Mgmt* **29**, 892–894.

DE BETHUNE, A. J. (1963) Child spacing, the mathematical probabilities, *Science* **142**, 1629–1634.

DEEVEY, E. S. (1947) Life tables for natural populations of animals, *Q. Rev. Biol.* **22**, 283–314.

ESPINAS, A. (1877) *Sociétés Animales*, Librairie Félix Alcan, Paris. 3rd edn, 1924, p. 6.

ERHARDT, C. L. (1952) Reporting of foetal deaths in New York City, *Publ. Hlth Rep. Wash.* **67**, 1161–1167.

FRENCH, F. E. and BIERMAN, J. M. (1962) Probabilities of foetal mortality *Publ. Hlth Rep. Wash.* **77**, 835–847.

FÜRTH, R. (1952) Physics of social equilibrium, *Advmt Sci.* **8**, 429–434.

HENRY, L. (1958) Intervals between confinements in the absence of birth control, *Eugen. Q.* **5**(4), 200–211.

HENRY, L. (1965) French statistical research in natural fertility, *Public Health and Population Change*, edited by M. C. Sheps and J. C. Ridley, pp. 333–350, University of Pittsburgh Press.

HERTIG, A. T., ROCK, J., ADAMS, E. C. and MENKIN, M. C. (1959) A study of biologic wastage in early human pregnancy, *Pediatrics* **23**, part 2, 202–211.

HEUSER, C. H. and STREETER, G. L. (1941) Development of the macaque embryo, *Contr. Embryol.* **29**, 15–00.

HYRENIUS, H. (1965) Demographic simulation models with the aid of electronic computers, *U.N. World Population Conference*, Belgrade.

HYRENIUS, H. and ADOLFSSON, I. (1964) *A fertility simulation model*, Göteborg.

HYRENIUS, H., ADOLFSSON, I. and HOLMBERG, I. (1966) *Demographic models*, Göteborg.

KAHN, H. (1962) Multiple quadrature by Monte Carlo methods, *Mathematical Methods for Digital Computers*, edited by A. Ralston and R. S. Wilf, pp. 249–257, J. Wiley & Sons.

LAYNE, J. N. (1958) Reproductive characteristics of the gray fox in Southern Illinois, *J. Wildl. Mgmt* **22**, 157–163.

NEWCOMBE, H. B. (1965) The study of mutations and selections in human populations, *Eugen. Rev.* **57**, 109–125.

POTTER, R. G., WYON, J. B., PARKER, M. and GORDON, J. E. (1965) A case study of birth interval dynamics, *Popul. Studies*, **19**(1), 81–96.

PERRIN, E. B. and SHEPS, M. C. (1964) Human reproduction: a stochastic process, *Biometrics* **20**(1), 28–45.

RIDLEY, J. C. and SHEPS, M. C. (1966) An analytic simulation model of human reproduction with demographic and biological components, *Popul. Studies* **19**, 297–310.

SALBER, E. J., FEINLEIB, M. and MACMAHON, B. (1966). The duration of post partum amenorrhea, *Am. J. Epidem.* **82**(3), 347–358.

SHAPIRO, S., JONES, E. W. and DENSEN, P. M. (1962) A life table of pregnancy terminations and correlates of foetal loss, *Milbank Meml Fund q. Bull.* **40**(1), 7–45.

SHEPS, M. C. and PERRIN, E. B. (1964) The distribution of birth intervals under a class of stochastic fertility models, *Popul. Studies* **17**(3), 321–331.

SHEPS, M. C. and PERRIN, E. B. (1966) Further results from a human fertility model with a variety of pregnancy outcomes, *Hum. Biol.* **38**, 180–193.

SHEPS, M. C. and RIDLEY, J. C. (1965) Studying determinants of natality: quantitative estimates through a simulation model, *U.N. Population Conference*, Belgrade.

SHEPS, M. C., MENKEN, J. A., RIDLEY, J. C. and LINGNER, J. W. (1967) Birth intervals and artefacts, *Regional Population Conference*, Sydney.

WESTOFF, C. F., POTTER, R. G., SAGI, P. C. and MISHLER, E. G. (1961) *Family Growth in Metropolitan America*, p. 47, Princeton University Press.

MILLING MASSES AND OPEN SPACES

John I. Clarke

Department of Geography, University of Durham

In recent decades there has been a growing awareness of the startling increase in the rate of world population growth, and its effects upon human numbers. At the end of 1968 there were about 3500 million people living on earth, 70 million more than in the previous year, 500 million more than in 1960, nearly 1000 million more than at mid-century, and twice as many as during the first world war. Another thousand million should be added by 1983. During 1968 alone it is estimated that about 119 million babies were born and 49 million people died. In the present state of census enumeration and vital registration we cannot be sure about precise numbers and rates of increase, largely because of uncertainty about demographic conditions in the developing countries and particularly China, where estimates of the population total range from 700 to 950 million. Nevertheless, the evidence available indicates that the present rate of increase of world population is about 2·0 per cent per annum, more than three times that of the first two decades of this century, and twice as high as during the period 1930–50 (see Table 1).

Patterns of World Population Growth

The most rapid acceleration in the rate of increase has taken place since the second world war. By this time most of the advanced or developed countries had reached a stage of slow population growth through long-term declines in mortality and fertility bringing substantial reduction in natural increase of population. On the other hand, before the second world war, natural increase in the under-developed or developing countries was curbed by high mortality. Since 1945 most of the developed countries have enjoyed further

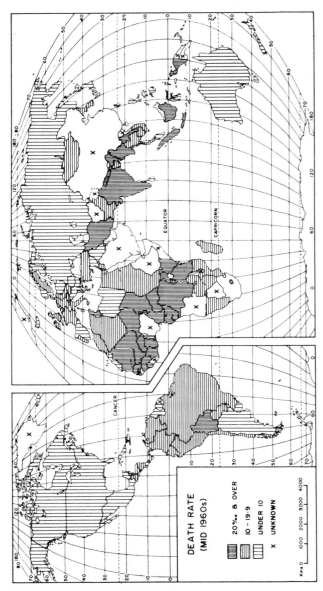

FIG. 1. *Death Rate (mid-1960's)*. The former contrasts in mortality between the developed and developing countries have been attenuated since the second world war by the rapid mortality declines in developing countries.

TABLE 1. Growth of World Population, 1950–1968

World Population (millions)		Average Annual Growth Rate (%)	
1750	791	1750–1800	0·4
1800	978	1800–1850	0·5
1850	1262	1850–1900	0·5
1900	1650	1900–1920	0·6
1920	1860	1920–1930	1·1
1930	2069	1930–1940	1·0
1940	2295	1940–1950	1·0
1950	2515	1950–1960	1·8
1960	2998	1960–1968	2·0
1968	3479		

Source: J. D. Durand, "The modern expansion of world population", *Proc. Am. Phil. Soc.*, vol. III, No. 3, June 1967, p. 136–59.

slight falls in mortality and have experienced rather higher fertility than during the inter-war years, and the result has been renewed growth. But this growth has been small in comparison with that occurring in many of the developing countries, which have benefited from the discoveries in medicine and hygiene by developed countries and have consequently experienced very rapid reductions in mortality. In many developing countries death rates have descended below 20 per thousand and in some below 10 per thousand (Fig. 1), but there has been no corresponding drop in fertility so birth rates are usually at least 35 per thousand and sometimes are as high as 55 per thousand (Fig. 2). In some countries the increased survival of young parents and children has even raised birth rates, causing more youthful age structures. In most developing countries more than 40 per cent of the population are under 15 years of age, and not unusually the percentage exceeds 45, in strong contrast with West European countries where less than 30 per cent are under 15 (Fig. 3). Only a few, small developing countries, like Hong Kong, Singapore and Puerto Rico, have experienced substantial fertility decline, and consequently fertility is one of the most useful socio-economic variables for distinguishing between developed and developing countries, although any distinction in a broad spectrum of social and economic development must inevitably be arbitrary.

One result of these contrasting growth patterns is that whereas the total population of the developing world, here crudely defined as Latin America, Africa and Asia (except Japan and the U.S.S.R.),

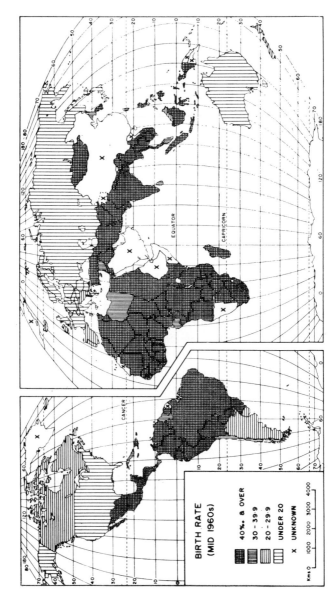

FIG. 2. *Birth Rate (mid-1960's)*. Birth rates are one of the best socio-economic criteria for distinguishing between developed and developing countries.

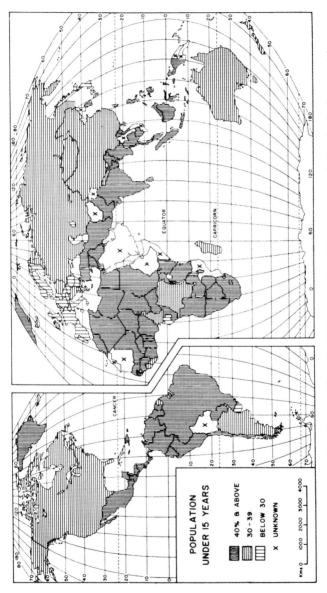

Fig. 3. *Population under 15 years.* Note the high proportions of young persons in the developing countries.

increased annually by 2·1 per cent between 1950 and 1965, the total population of the developed world grew by only 1·2 per cent per annum. During this period the developing world accounted for 78 per cent of world population growth, and by 1965 contained 70 per cent of the total population. That proportion is increasing continually, although within the developing world there is a wide variety of growth rates (Fig. 4) depending largely on the interplay of the two variables, fertility and mortality. The highest rates, above 3·0 per cent per annum, are found in much of tropical Latin America and some of the smaller countries of Africa and Asia, where high and sometimes rising fertility is accompanied by low or declining mortality. At the end of this century the population of Latin America may be more than ten times as large as at the beginning, but this rapid Latin American increase does not involve such mammoth numbers as in Asia which already contains 56 per cent of mankind, a proportion which is growing annually. Of the 70 million extra people on earth this year, most are Asians, especially Chinese, Indians, Pakistanis and Indonesians. We must remind ourselves that China with about 750 million contains more people than the whole of Europe, and India with 523 millions has more than all the Americas and about as many as the combined populations of the three southern continents.

Changing Patterns of Population Distribution

At the moment, the map of world population distribution (Fig. 5) offers little correlation with the map of population growth, because most of those areas now experiencing rapid growth have known this condition for only a short time, some for only a few years. The present distribution map reflects more the momentum of past distributions of population, in particular three overlapping phases:

(1) pre-industrial times, characterized by concentration of population in Eurasia;
(2) nineteenth century expansion of Europeans overseas;
(3) the twentieth century, characterized by rapid growth and urbanization of population along with inertia in the overall pattern of world population distribution.

Estimates of pre-censal populations have only low reliability, but if we accept the latest estimates by J. D. Durand (1967), we find that about 1750, prior to the industrial revolution, some 63 per cent of the

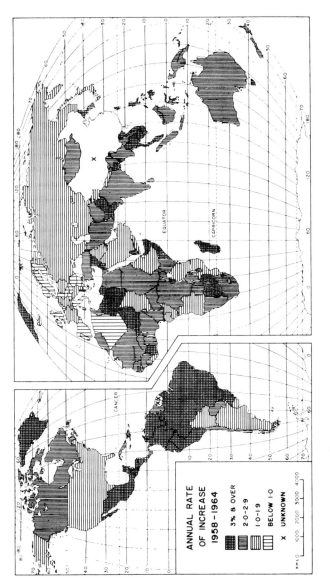

FIG. 4. *Annual Rate of Increase, 1958–1964.* Developing countries experience the most rapid rates of increase.

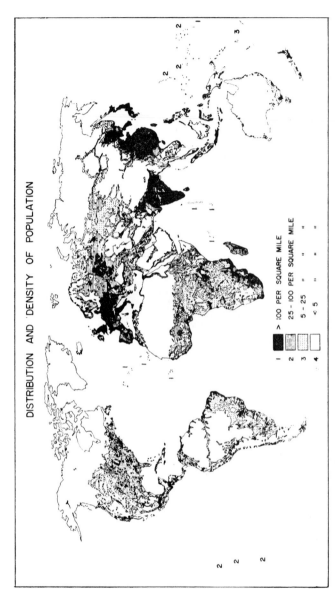

FIG. 5. *The World Distribution and Density of Population*. Simplified from *The Times Atlas of the World*. Source: J. I. Clarke, *Population Geography*, 1965, p. 15.

world's population of 791 million (see Table 2) lived in Asia and 84 per cent in Eurasia, where the main civilizations had encouraged the organization of mankind in settled communities based upon cultivation.

TABLE 2. Medium Estimates of Growth of Population in Continents, 1750–2000

| | (Population in millions) | | | | | |
	1750	1800	1850	1900	1950	2000
World	791	978	1262	1650	2515	6130
Asia	498	630	801	925	1381	3458
Europe	125	152	208	296	392	527
U.S.S.R.	42	56	76	134	180	353
North America	2	7	26	82	166	354
Latin America	16	24	38	74	162	638
Africa	106	107	111	133	222	768
Oceania	2	2	2	6	13	32

Source: J. D. Durand, *op. cit.*, p. 137.

The largest concentrations of population were to be found in China (200 million), the Indian subcontinent (190 million) and Europe (167 million), which together contained 70 per cent of the world's population on 18 per cent of the land area. Here were propitious combinations of environmental conditions, food crops, land use systems, old established cultures, and periods of political stability. The densest populations prevailed in lowland areas where heat and water supplies enabled high yield cereal crops to be grown intensively, as in many of the valleys and deltas of East and South Asia. In Europe the climate was less conducive but a wide variety of food crops thrived, and European commercial and industrial propensities were growing. Outside of Eurasia, the only continent with a sizeable population (over 100 million) in the mid-eighteenth century was Africa, but its numbers had been drastically curbed by slavery and disease as well as by the physical inhospitability of large areas of desert and tropical forest. The New World and Oceania were only very scantily peopled.

During the late eighteenth and nineteenth centuries, the unique civilization of Europe culminated in a remarkable development of industry and commerce encouraging the growth of populations, their concentration into cities and their spread to the more temperate parts of other continents where indigenous peoples were sparse or absent. The relatively empty continents of the Americas, Australasia and Africa as well as Asiatic Russia were taken over during the nineteenth century by Europeans, who gained political control of immense expanses of the world, but settled and established themselves in fairly localized areas. In colonized countries like the United States, Canada, Argentina, Uruguay, South Africa, Algeria, Australia and New Zealand they mostly settled in coastal cities or farmed large areas at low densities. Their population distribution was extremely uneven and largely peripheral, and these patterns have prevailed. North America, which now has 220 million people largely of European extraction, has evolved as a primary concentration of humanity, and in Latin America Europeans have contributed massively to its present pattern of population clusters, to its racial amalgam and to its population growth. European expansion to Australia and New Zealand came later, reducing and then numerically overwhelming the small indigenous populations, although these countries have never received migration streams of Europeans comparable in size to those entering North America or even Latin America.

During the twentieth century the large-scale migration of Europeans has been staunched. Most of the overseas European offshoots now have policies which impede large-scale immigration of other populations, especially those from developing countries of Asia for whom migration might have acted as a safety valve. Consequently, the nineteenth century process of population redistribution as between continents has been partially arrested, and great unevenness of population distribution at continental level persists. Despite recent rapid population growth, the "empty continents" (the Americas, Africa and Oceania) contain less than one-quarter of mankind, while Eurasia still contains over three-quarters.

There seems little likelihood that those continents which are relatively empty will be populated by Asians, or even by large waves of Europeans. In other words, the superimposition of an irregular mesh of political boundaries over the earth's surface has had a stabilizing influence upon world population distribution. Boundaries have become barriers to human movement, through immigration restrictions and quotas and political differences. The trend during this century has been toward a decline in the significance of international migrations in contrast with the growing significance of natural increase. Populations and their relation to resources have become nationalized. Some would argue, therefore, that it is fanciful to speak of a world population problem or a world food supply, when the political divisions of mankind impede the free movement of men and materials and encourage growing disparities in levels of economic development and standards of living. In the present political climate, solutions to most population pressures must be solved within national boundaries; international migration is only likely to alter substantially the population size of small or micro-states, like Kuwait, Israel, Eire or Trinidad. It is most unlikely to affect greatly the population size of macro-states, seven of which contained in 1968 at least 58 per cent of the total world population: China with approximately 750 million, India 523, U.S.S.R. 289, U.S.A. 201, Pakistan 126, Indonesia 113 and Japan 101. So popula-tion size may influence population dynamics, and not merely through migration but also because it is easier, generally speaking, to effect rapidly mortality decline (and probably fertility decline as well) in small states or islands than in large states, where more complex ecosystems and cultural patterns prevail. Islands are particularly prone to demographic instability.

It follows from these remarks that during the later part of the twentieth century political boundaries and patterns of natural increase will probably have a growing influence upon the map of world population distribution, unless there can be more progress toward international unity.

Urban and Rural Populations

The twentieth century is also witnessing massive urbanization, which is intensifying the unevenness of world population distri-bution. The rate of urbanization is many times greater than that of world population growth (see Table 3).

At the beginning of this century less than one in ten lived in towns with 20,000 or more inhabitants; by 1960 more than one in four did so, although the high levels of urbanization in nearly all the developed countries contrasted with the lower levels prevailing in developing countries (Fig. 6). If the present rate of urbanization persists, more than half of the world's inhabitants will live in towns by the end of this century, and Kingsley Davis (1965) has even suggested that eventually 85–95 per cent of the world's population may well be living in towns; in other words, the situation which now prevails in Britain may become the norm.

TABLE 3. Growth in World Urban Population, 1800–1960
(Population in millions)

	Total Population	Population in Localities of 20,000 and over		Population in Localities of 100,000 and over		Rural population	
		Number	%	Number	%	Number	%
1800	906	22	2·4	16	1·8	884	97·6
1850	1171	50	4·3	28	2·4	1121	95·7
1900	1608	148	9·2	89	5·5	1460	90·8
1950	2400	502	20·9	314	13·1	1898	79·1
1960	2962	803	27·1	590	19·9	2159	72·9

Source: G. Breese, *Urbanization in Newly Developing Countries*, Prentice-Hall, 1966, p. 19.

Most town-dwellers live in large cities. In 1960, nearly three-quarters of all town-dwellers lived in large cities with 100,000 or more inhabitants (see Table 4).

TABLE 4. Rural and Urban Populations by Continent, 1960
(Population in millions)

	Rural areas and villages with less than 2000–5000 inhabitants		2000 to 5000–99,000 inhabitants		100,000 inhabitants and over	
	Number	%	Number	%	Number	%
North America	31	16	47	24	119	60
Latin America	116	55	41	20	51	25
Europe	298	46	152	24	189	30
Asia	1296	79	151	9	204	12
Africa	213	85	18	7	20	8
Oceania	6	37	3	19	7	44
World Total ...	1960	66	412	14	590	20

Source: H. Hoyt, *World Urbanization: Expanding Population in a Shrinking World*, Urban Land Institute Technical Bulletin No. 43 (Washington D.C.), Table 16, p. 49.

The United Nations *Demographic Yearbook* for 1966 lists 1505 such cities and 113 with more than one million inhabitants (Mountjoy, 1968). Homer Hoyt (1963) has estimated that 42 per cent of the world's population will be living in cities with 100,000 or more inhabitants by 2000 A.D., and one-fifth in cities with one million or

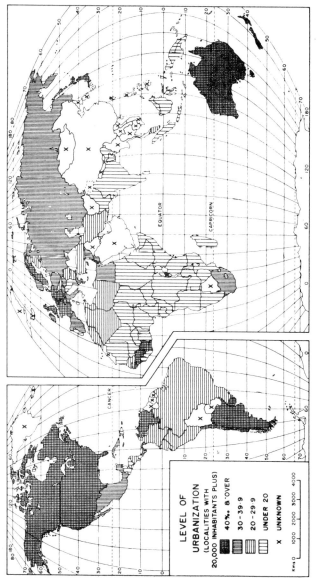

Fig. 6. *Level of Urbanization* (localities with 20,000 inhabitant plus). At present the contrast between developed and developing countries is marked, but it is diminishing.

more inhabitants. Conurbations and urbanized regions will contain a growing proportion of the world's town-dwellers, further concentrating population distribution. And it should be mentioned that few countries are exempt from this growing trend toward urbanization. Despite this trend, the world's rural population is growing fast. Such is the speed of population growth that in 1968 there were almost certainly as many people living in rural areas as in the whole world in 1950. The patterns of urban and rural population distribution and growth are not coincident, for there are still highly populous countries like Indonesia and Pakistan, which are feebly urbanized. Most of these new rural dwellers are Asians, for Asia contains nearly two-thirds of the world's rural population, Europe and Africa together containing about one-quarter. If the world rural population continues to grow at the rates expected by Hoyt, it will not be far short of 2900 million by 2000 A.D., or nearly as many as the total world population of 1960.

The Inhabited Area

These growing urban and rural populations pose the problem of the uneven occupation of the earth's surface and the utilization of its resources. Four-fifths of mankind live on one-fifth of its land area. The unevenness is particularly apparent latitudinally; nearly four-fifths live in the temperate zones of the northern hemisphere between 20° and 60°N, over one-tenth between the equator and 20°N, under one-tenth in the southern hemisphere and less than one-half per cent north of 60°N. The three most obvious concentrations of population are in

(a) south and east Asia (including China, Japan, Indonesia, India and Pakistan), which contain over half of the world's population;
(b) Europe, with one-fifth; and
(c) the north-eastern part of the United States and adjacent areas in Canada, with about 5 per cent of the world's population.

These three concentrations comprise over three-quarters of mankind.

The inhabited area, sometimes known as the ecumene, is of course much more extensive, but despite the massive redistribution of population over the last two centuries, there have been few major advances in the ecumene. Still only one-tenth of the earth's land surface is currently used as arable land and less than one-fifth as permanent meadows and pastures. At present, only about three-tenths of the land area is permanently inhabited, the precise proportion depending on what level of population density one takes as a threshold of habitation; it is obvious that small groups can exist almost anywhere in the world, but they have little influence upon the general pattern of the inhabited area.

Within the ecumene the patterns of population density are influenced by multiple environmental, cultural, political and economic factors, but perhaps the most significant is the type of economy, in particular the contrast between subsistence and commercial economies. In subsistence economies, populations are largely rural and densities are directly related to the intensity of agriculture and thus are indirectly related to the environment, whereas in commercial economies the importance of the environment is greatly diminished.

Climate and Population Distribution

Some seven-tenths of the earth's land surface are sparsely inhabited or uninhabited. Despite the irregular nature of man's expansion over the earth's surface, these are mostly areas which to a greater or lesser extent have proved hostile or negative environments for human occupation, and in particular experience extreme climatic conditions which are difficult for human existence. In general terms, they mainly comprise the hot and mid-latitude deserts, the polar and sub-polar lands, the tropical wet lands and the high mountains.

All these areas pose severe climatic problems to human survival, but it must be realised that absolute environmental limitations to human existence are few. Pastoral nomads have learnt to live in deserts, Eskimos in polar lands and Andean Indians at high altitudes. Among such peoples the physical environment has a direct impact upon man, influencing his physiology, psychology, vital rates and modes of life. Among peoples with more advanced cultures, however, the effects of the physical environment are diminished, especially in cities. Certainly, it would be wrong to overstress the physiological problems of living in these areas, and to forget that they present special climatic problems for cultivation, afforestation, livestock rearing, road and rail construction, water supply, sewage disposal and many other aspects of life. The solutions found for temperate climates are not always suitable for more hostile areas. It may also be argued that the problems of the settlement of large numbers in such climatic areas are quite different from those of small groups, because climate is not the only challenge. Peoples from advanced societies find that difficult climatic environments are not only physiologically unattractive, but thay are costly to develop. Costs are a major deterrent unless there is some great inducement, such as mineral wealth, power resources or (in desert areas) water supply. In some parts of the world where population pressure is high, there is a real need to occupy difficult environments; elsewhere the need does not arise. Consequently, it is not wise to generalize too much about the relationships between climate and population density on a world scale.

One of the difficulties in analysing such a relationship is that of classifying climates, which are merely average weather conditions, and, unlike human populations, are not composed of discrete units. Consequently, they are not divisible by sharp lines; nobody can define accurately the edge of a desert or a tundra. So any classification of climates is arbitrary. It follows, therefore, that various classifications by Köppen, de Martonne, Trewartha, Thornthwaite and others can only be regarded as broad guides to the pattern of world climates. There is no universally acceptable definition of a desert, or of the humid tropics, so it is possible to have a variety of analyses of population distribution according to climatic types. Staszewski's (1961) analysis of world population in 1950 in relation to Köppen's climatic classification is just one example, and therefore should be treated with caution (see Table 5).

Another reason for regarding such data with reservations is that elements of the physical environment do not act in isolation, but are essentially interrelated; environments are wholes. If we examine the influence of climate by itself, we are neglecting the intimate areal association of surface features, water, vegetation and soil with climate. Preston James (1966) emphasises this association in his examination of 9 habitat regions, for which he has also calculated the percentage distribution of population (see Table 6).

Many find these habitat regions, in which climate plays a vital role, more meaningful than climatic regions, which are more abstract and intangible. Nevertheless, it must be remembered that these broad categories also mask a host of minor variations.

TABLE 5. World Population Distribution (c 1950) in Relation to
Köppen's Climatic Classification

	Type of Climate	Area (%)	Population (%)	Average Density (p. sq. km.)
1.	Tropical rainy	8·1	8·0	18·4
2.	Savanna	13·8	10·7	14·4
3.	Steppe	15·6	6·7	7·9
4.	Desert	13·2	1·4	1·9
5.	Warm, dry winter	8·4	27·6	61·1
6.	Warm, dry summer	2·0	4·4	41·1
7.	Cool temperate	6·5	20·7	60·3
8.	Continental, cold winter ...	18·1	14·5	15·0
9.	Continental cold dry winter	5·4	5·7	19·8
10, 11.	Tundra, Polar, Tibet ...	8·9	0·3	—
		100·0	100·0	18·6

Source: J. Staszewski, "Bevölkerungsverteilung nach den Klimagebeiten von W. Köppen", *Petermanns Geogr. Mitteilungen*, vol. 105, 1961, pp. 133-8.

TABLE 6. Percentage World Population Distribution (c 1963) in
Relation to James's Habitat Regions

		Area %	Population %
1.	Dry Lands	18	6
2.	Tropical Forest Lands	10	28
3.	Tropical Woodlands and Savannas ...	17	5
4.	Mediterranean Woodlands	1	5
5.	Mid-Latitude Mixed Forest Lands ...	7	42
6.	Mid-Latitude Grasslands	9	7
7.	Boreal Forest Lands	10	Negligible
8.	Polar Lands	16	Negligible
9.	Mountain Lands	12	7
		100	100

Source: P. James, *A Geography of Man* 3rd ed., 1966, p. 23.

With these remarks in mind, it is now pertinent to sketch in the broad outlines of the main negative areas (see Fig. 7).

The Negative Areas

The cold lands of the Arctic, Subarctic and Antarctic cover about one-quarter of the earth's land surface but support a negligible proportion of its population. The distribution of the cold regions

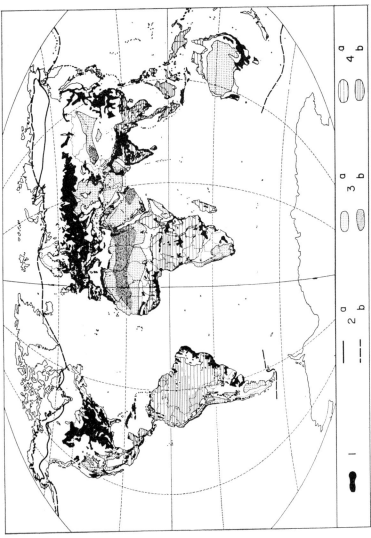

FIG. 7. *Frontiers of Agriculture. Legend* (1). Extent of cultivated land. (2) Cold frontier—(a) southern limit of permanently frozen soils, and (b) poleward limits of forest. (3) Arid frontier—(a) arid lands, and (b) extremely arid lands. (4) Humid tropical frontier—(a) more or less periodically wet lands, and (b) more

is not only determined by latitude; it is considerably influenced by the disposition and shape of the continental land masses, and as climatic conditions tend to deteriorate from west to east along any line of latitude in the northern part of the northern hemisphere the eastern sides of continents are less populous than the western sides. In many of these cold regions the average temperature of the warmest month does not reach 10°C, it never stops freezing for 7 to 10 months each year and strong winds are prevalent, so human beings find great difficulty in mobilizing the means of existence. Indeed, there is little doubt that prolonged cold is the greatest deterrent to large-scale human occupation, not only because it prevents cultivation except under artificial conditions, but also because of its physiological effects. In general, the cold regions offer little prospect for widespread settlement on a scale capable of alleviating heavy population pressures, although in Northern Canada, Alaska and Soviet Asia it has been shown technically possible to settle millions of persons in cities provided with their own artificial environments. Political differences, however, make it seem unlikely that Soviet Asia will welcome in the near future peoples from the densely populated countries of South and East Asia; at present it is only encouraging settlers from European Russia.

Cold is also one of the factors discouraging human concentration in high mountains, along with reduction in atmospheric and oxygen pressures, steep slopes, exposure and ruggedness. All play an important part in restricting human access, habitation and cultivation in mountain regions. In general, high altitudes tend to be very sparsely peopled; just over four-fifths of the world's population live below 500 metres above sea-level (see Table 7), and only one in twelve

TABLE 7. Percentage World Population (c 1945) in Relation to Altitude

Continent	Elevation above Sea Level (in metres)			
	under 200	200–500	500–1000	Over 1000
World	56·2	24·0	11·6	8·2
Europe	68·8	23·5	7·2	0·5
Asia	56·5	23·5	11·7	8·3
Africa	32·4	24·1	20·8	22·7
North America ...	46·9	33·3	7·9	11·9
South America ...	42·3	15·0	22·8	19·9
Australia	72·9	17·8	8·4	0·9

Source: J. Staszewski, "Vertical distribution of world population", *Polish Academy of Sciences, Geographical Studies*, No. 14, 1957, p. 18.

lives on the 21·5 per cent of the earth's surface lying above 1000 metres (Staszewski, 1957).

On the other hand, the influence of altitude upon human habitat is closely related to latitudinal position. In lower latitudes mountains are frequently more attractive climatically than low-lying areas, which are hotter and often more infested with disease. Most high altitude dwellers live in the middle or low latitudes of Latin America, Africa or Asia, especially in Mexico, the Andean countries, Ethiopia, East Africa, and countries along the Alpine-Himalayan mountain areas. The highest levels of extensive settlement are found in Bolivia, where hundreds of thousands live above 4000 metres, and the city of La Paz at 3620 metres has nearly 400,000 inhabitants. In the Himalayas and Mexico, settlements exist over 5000 metres—more than twice the height of Mexico City, where the 1968 Olympic Games were held—but at this altitude the constraints of low atmospheric and oxygen pressures begin to become acute. There can be little doubt that many mountain zones at lesser elevations in low latitudes offer greater opportunities for increased human occupation, as for example in East Africa, but it must be said that many mountains are experiencing downhill movement or depopulation, especially those which have acted as havens of refuge for oppressed minorities, as in the Middle East and Africa. Moreover, it is unlikely that increased occupation of high altitudes would radically transform the pattern of the ecumene.

Some people suggest that the arid areas offer the greatest potential for extension of the ecumene, and even portray a fantastic future for the arid lands. St. Barbe Baker (1966) for example, goes so far as to say that the Sahara is potentially the richest zone on earth, capable of containing "homes and gardens for 3850 million people", more than the present world total population. Aridity is most evident in the hot and mid-latitude deserts, which again cover about one-fifth of the earth's surface, and suffer from variability of precipitation, high temperature ranges and desiccating winds. Here water shortage has been overcome by indigenous peoples in a variety of ways, notably by nomadic forms of life associated with sparse population densities and by irrigated agriculture associated with high population densities on limited areas and using water either from rivers passing through deserts (e.g. the Nile) or from underground sources. A number of methods have been used to obtain such underground water, some traditional (e.g. qanats, wells) and some modern (e.g.

artesian wells, pumps). The great densities of population which exist wherever water is available in large quantities, as well as technical progress in the discovery of water, distillation of sea-water, artificial rain-making, dry farming, afforestation and adaptation of plant species have all encouraged a reassessment of the utility of arid environments. Many authorities agree that they offer sound prospects for increased settlements, but this largely depends upon water supply and the exploitation of mineral wealth, and therefore settlement will probably be more clustered than widespread. The recent changes associated with massive developments of the oil industry in sparsely populated desert countries like Libya, Kuwait and Saudi Arabia support this generalization. In these countries urbanization is growing rapidly, and the impact of the climate upon man is diminishing in air-conditioned city environments.

Unlike the cold, the high and the arid lands, the humid tropics cannot be considered as entirely hostile. For one thing they vary substantially in physical conditions, the most notable contrast being between the tropical forest lands with rainfall in all seasons and the tropical woodlands and savannas where there is a season of moisture deficiency. The disparity in the human occupance of those two types of physical environment is great; while the tropical forests occupy only one-tenth of the earth's surface they contain over one-quarter of its population, the tropical woodlands and savannas comprise 17 per cent of the area but contain only 5 per cent of the population. The disparities are even greater when one compares different regions of the world; while large, long-settled agricultural countries in Asia and small islands with plantation economies have some of the highest population densities in the world, hot, wet lands in parts of South-East Asia, Central Africa and South America are sparsely peopled or uninhabited. Epitomizing this contrast is the fact that there are more people on the island of Java in Indonesia than in the vast Amazon and Congo basins put together. It is true that these areas do not have precisely similar physical conditions, but physical differences alone are not enough to explain such contrasts in human occupation; the answer lies more in the history of human settlement in the various parts of the humid tropics. Although all parts of the humid tropics offer obstacles to human occupation—parasites, diseases, vegetational and microbial exuberance, soil leaching and infertility, torrential rainfall and flooding—

the physiological difficulties of living in such climates, and their monotony have been often exaggerated. Indeed, as many tropical diseases come under control the humid tropics become quite desirable places to live, even for white people. This increase in the habitability of the tropics makes it easier to tackle the problems of economic development, but habitability is a long way from habitation.

Habitability

Large areas of the earth's surface have long been devoid of human population concentrations, but this does not mean that they are perpetually committed to this state. The value and utilization of environments change over time; we only have to look at the English downlands to see that this is true. The same downlands also exemplify the fact that environments may be variously regarded and utilized by peoples of different cultural traditions. In Africa, we also find ample evidence of the diverse ways that African and European peoples have perceived and used similar environments, with wide contrasts in resulting population distributions and densities. Indeed, population distributions rarely accord completely with physical potential—they also respond to a host of human influences, notably the character and scale of economic activities. Visitors to North America note the low population densities and productivity of physical environments which would attract much higher densities in other parts of the world. The fact is that environmental potential is not enough to ensure human occupancy; many social, economic and political factors come into play.

Geographers are also aware that environmental potential cannot easily be quantified, nor can optimum population density be easily determined. They depend so much upon technological advance and human ideals, which vary greatly from one part of the world to another. In this context it is worthwhile recalling Ackerman's (1967) five-fold classification of the world according to population/ resource ratios and the availability of technology:

(1) One-sixth of the world's population live in technology-source areas with high population-resource ratios, where industrialization and technology enable an extension of the resources through world trade. Western Europe and Japan are the prime examples.

very useful basis for actuarial work but it became clear in the early part of this century that it was not universally applicable, particularly at the older ages where accumulating data suggested a slowing down of the rate of increase with age. In 1932 Wilfred Perks put forward further modifications of the Gompertz form and extensive calculations (Beard, 1951a) have shown that these provide very reasonable mathematical expressions of rates of mortality for a wide range of experiences.

8. The simplest member of the Perks's family is the logistic and the relationship between the three named curves can be briefly expressed as:

$$\mu_x = Bc^x \qquad \text{(Gompertz)},$$
$$\mu_x = A + Bc^x \qquad \text{(Makeham)},$$
$$\mu_x = A + Bc^x/(1 + Dc^x) \quad \text{(Perks)}.$$

These formulae are, of course, applicable to adult mortality only.

9. If the deaths in a life table are looked upon as a frequency distribution then μ_x is the ratio of the ordinate at age x to the tail area above age x. For a very wide range of frequency distributions this function is of sigmoid form and it is not apparent whether the satisfactory representation of μ_x by a logistic (Perks) curve is because the formula has a theoretical significance or because it provides a good approximation to the particular function of a family of frequency curves which can be used to represent the distribution of deaths by age. Furthermore, apart from a few elementary cases, the ratio of the ordinate to the tail area is a complicated mathematical function. In seeking to describe this function (i.e. μ_x) by a simple mathematical form it may be that attention is being directed towards the wrong function and more progress in the understanding of mortality might be achieved by studying the curve of deaths (d_x or μl_x).

10. Karl Pearson (1897) did, of course, render a description of the curve of deaths as the sum of five different frequency curves and other writers, e.g. Phillips (1954), have endeavoured to encourage study of this function. In his 1932 paper Perks suggested that it might be worth while studying $d \log \mu l_x/dx$, i.e. the function which has the same mathematical relationship to μl_x as μ_x has to l_x and Ogborn (1953) did some related work but systematic studies are lacking.

11. The observed feature that a wide range of adult human

mortality tables could be expressed by the logistic curve prompted me to consider models in which the population was assumed to be heterogeneous and my first efforts were directed to deterministic forms in which the population was assumed to be stratified with common mortality rates. If $\mu_k{}^s$ is the force of mortality at time ($\equiv$ age) k for the group with "longevity" factor s and $\phi(s)/ds$ is the proportion of the initial population with factor s, then the mortality rate at time k for the whole population is:

$$\mu_k = \frac{\int \phi(s)\mu_k{}^s \exp\left(-\int_0^k \mu_t{}^s \, dt\right) ds}{\int \phi(s) \exp\left(-\int_0^k \mu_t{}^s \, dt\right) ds},$$

where the integrals are taken over the whole range of s.

12. If it be assumed that $\mu_k{}^s = \alpha + \beta s \exp(\lambda k)$, i.e. a Makeham form, and that $\phi(s) = \kappa s^p \exp(-\gamma s)$ $(0 \leqslant s < \infty)$, i.e. a Gamma distribution, then

$$\mu_k = \alpha + \frac{(p+1)\beta \exp(\lambda k)}{(\gamma\lambda - \beta) + \beta \exp(\lambda k)},$$

which is a logistic form (Beard, 1959).

13. Whilst the foregoing provides an interesting mathematical description of a process which leads to a logistic form it suffers from the disadvantage that it assumes that the mortality of the various strata is Makeham in form for which experimental verification seems very difficult. It is also a deterministic model and implies that each individual in the population has a unique "longevity" tag; whilst studies of heredity have shown correlations, the model does not seem to lend itself to development.

14. Concurrently with these ideas I was also thinking about the so-called "shot" models. In these it is assumed that individuals accumulate "shots" from random firings and are assumed to be dead when the total reaches a given figure. Forward models of this type did not lead to numerical results which fitted the facts. There are however "backward" models in which shots are lost and death is assumed to occur when the starting stock has been reduced to a given level and I found that this type of model did lead to sensible numerical results.

15. For example if it be assumed that $l_t{}^\alpha$ are the number of persons alive at time t with α units remaining and that the chance of losing a unit in the next interval is pdt times the number of units remaining then we can write:

$$\frac{dl_t{}^\alpha}{dt} = -p\alpha l_t{}^\alpha + p(\alpha+1)l_t{}^{\alpha+1}.$$

The solution to this equation is $l_t{}^\alpha = \binom{r}{\alpha} \exp(-p\alpha t)[1 - \exp(-pt)]^{r-\alpha}$, where r is the initial stock of units. If the initial population is so distributed that the proportion with stock r is $D/(1+D)^{r-\alpha+1}$, then it can be shown that the overall mortality will be:

$$\mu_t = \frac{p\alpha D \exp(pt)}{1 + D \exp(pt)},$$

i.e. a logistic form (Beard, 1964).

16. The deaths at time t for a given stratum are $p\alpha l_t{}^\alpha$ and the force of mortality is:

$$\mu_t{}^\alpha = \frac{p\alpha l_t{}^\alpha}{\sum\limits_\alpha l_t{}^\alpha} \times \frac{p\alpha l_t{}^\alpha}{\displaystyle\int_t^\infty p\alpha l_s{}^\alpha \, ds}.$$

For the form $l_t{}^\alpha$ derived in paragraph 15 these expressions cannot be evaluated in simple terms although it may be noted that $l_t{}^\alpha$ can be expressed as a Beta ordinate (Pearson Type I) with a logarithmic transformation. For this curve $\mu_t{}^\alpha$ will have a sigmoid form. This is not without interest as it suggests that the curve of deaths could be fitted with a Pearson type function subject to a change of variable.

17. One series of experiments I made was to use the Γ function for actuarial calculations (Beard, 1950, 1952) and some earlier unpublished work on fitting Pearson curves to the curve of deaths with a transformed variable gave encouraging results, but were not followed up.

18. From the foregoing two distinct models have been found which lead to the logistic form for the force of mortality, the first is a stratified population with the strata subject to Makeham mortality and the second is a different stratification but with mortality dependent on the state of "deterioration" reached at time ($\equiv$ age) t by a purely random process. These two models are reminiscent of the accident models in which the negative binomial distribution,

which describes so well the accident distribution, can be shown to arise from a number of different underlying models. In the mortality case the logistic may well be playing a similar role to the negative binomial.

19. The important point is, however, the fact that the purely random process model, provided the backward form is used, does lead to logistic values of the force of mortality which are actually found from statistical observations. The model implies that individuals start their life with a total quantity of "units" which diminishes throughout life on a probability basis, i.e. the chance that a unit is lost in a given interval is solely governed by the quantity remaining at the time. The backward model does not give a Gompertz form as a solution (except as a limiting form) but since the essential difference between the logistic and Gompertz forms is at the highest ages it is necessary to consider the data in this region before ruling out the logistic model.

20. The Gompertz model implies that μ_x continues to increase indefinitely with x whereas the logistic implies a limiting value. So far as human data are concerned there seems little firm data to work on. If a population is considered there is plenty of evidence that the increase in the rate of mortality slackens off at the older ages but this could be due, of course, to selective processes in which weaker members are the first to die (i.e. the first stratified model). The slackening of the increase in μ_x in the second model comes from the reduction in "resistance" by the random process until most survivors are within one unit of death. My own preference is to accept that there is an upper limit to μ_x; the evidence from actuarial sources of "damaged" lives (Beard, 1951b) is also interesting as the numerical values derived from select tables are in line with those derived by fitting a logistic formula to the adult age range.

21. However, the evidence may be studied from another angle. If the curve of deaths is regarded as the critical function, the discrimination between a logistic and a Gompertz form will depend on the few survivors at the tail of the curve. About 1% of births survive beyond age 90 or so and it would require a great deal of data to sort out the difference between the logistic and Gompertz distribution for the tail. Too close attention to the rates in this region may obscure the reliability of the data in terms of the overall observations.

22. So far, of course, the foregoing has been concerned with the

mortality observed from groups of individuals and the suggestion reached is that the mortality process is best defined in terms of deterioration of the individuals within the group by a random process. However, we know that individuals vary in regard to their expected longevity and susceptibility to different causes of death. To extend the model means that the notion of homogeneity must be dropped and allowance made for variations between individuals.

23. Before generalizing in this way I would refer to some ideas I tried in seeking a link between cellular processes and deterioration processes (Beard, 1960/1961a, 1961b). These were not particularly profitable but they were formative, particularly the statistical work on causes of death.

24. The animal organism is a highly complex and interlocking assembly of sub-systems, each of which is ultimately resolvable in biochemical terms. In principle it would seem reasonable to assume that the process of living is ultimately expressible in physical terms, although any relationship found would necessarily be complicated Mortality is one extreme of the process of living and the study of mortality can be regarded as a limiting case of the study of the living organism. Although the various sub-systems are interlocked the feature that the behaviour of the aggregate can be described as a purely random process is a temptation to postulate that the sub-systems could also be so described.

25. Instead of attempting to analyse the various sub-systems a statistical approach would be to group the various causes of death according to their observed distributions and examine the resulting groups to see whether the particular mortality patterns did lead to different stochastic models. Following on this line of thought, my first experiment was to take the deaths by causes in England and Wales for 1958 (Registrar General) and group those causes which showed similar distributions of death by age. It was appreciated that this was a purely statistical exercise as the distribution of deaths is that arising from the particular population distribution at the time and that the underlying mortality rates were dependent rates.

26. The Pearson moment coefficients were calculated from these distributions (males and females separately) and attention was restricted to causes of death which might reasonably be regarded as constitutional in nature. The $\sqrt{\beta_1}, \beta_2$ values were then plotted on a chart which I had calculated to delineate the areas where the logistic fell. With one exception (cancer of the breast, female, which appeared

to be a "mixture") all the points fell within the logistic area, although, of course, the parameters differed from cause to cause.

27. Incidentally the $\sqrt{\beta_1}, \beta_2$ chart had been calculated to facilitate studies on mortality generally. There are growing numbers of series of observations on various animals and it seemed that the easiest method of obtaining a quick view of the form of the mortality was to calculate the moments of the distribution by ages at death and enter these on the chart. This technique handles the statistical significance problems arising from the limited number of observations in such series which tend to be obscured if attempts are made to estimate rates of mortality directly from the data.

28. The proper next stage in experimentation would have been to calculate for each of the (grouped) causes of death, independent rates of mortality and from them independent curves of death. This I did not do although some limited calculations were made to confirm that it was reasonable to expect the logistic to hold in the independent case. At this stage my attention was also drawn to the work by Prawitz (1954) who had used the idea of calculating independent rates by causes for use in forecasting mortality. More recent work in this field has been done by Chiang (1960).

29. However, at this time (1961) the controversy about smoking and lung cancer was becoming very active and it seemed worth while looking at the population data to see if the ideas had any application in this field. My idea was that if the increase in lung cancer was primarily associated with cigarette smoking then the mortality process might be expressed as a random process. This would also provide a difficult case on which to test the techniques.

30. The results have been described elsewhere (Beard, 1963) and will not be repeated here. The first job was to collate the relevant statistics and for this purpose the General Register Office Studies on Medical and Population Subject No. 13, provided the information in a convenient form. Consideration of the variations in the (independent) central rates of mortality for cancer of the lung showed that it was possible to find a reasonable representation of the data over the years 1913 to 1958 and for ages 27 to 82 by a product formula of the type:

$$\mu_x^T = k\phi(T-x)\chi(T)f(x),$$

where $\phi(T-x)$ is a function dependent on year of birth, $\chi(T)$ a function dependent on the calendar year of experience and $f(x)$ a function solely dependent on age. This, of course, is a descriptive formula.

31. However, if the hypothesis of a purely physical cause for this mortality held then it would be reasonable to expect the $f(x)$ function to be similar for males and females. After some experiments it was, in fact, found possible to find a set of values in which the k factors and the $f(x)$ functions were similar for males and females, provided the ϕ factor was related to the proportion of smokers in the generation and the χ factor related to the quantity of cigarettes smoked in the various calendar years, but with a time lag of about 15 years.

32. The critics can, of course, argue that this descriptive model still only reflects statistical association but there is one other piece of evidence to support the hypothesis. If the mortality rates $f(x)$ have a purely physical basis then it would be reasonable to expect them to be described by a stochastic process of some type. First attempts at this were unsuccessful but a careful study of the basic data showed that the frequency distributions of the deaths from lung cancer had patterns very suggestive that they were composed of deaths with distributions of two different types. No information is available to classify the population deaths according to the type of cancer but by making use of some Norwegian data (Kreyberg, 1962) and splitting the deaths into two series it was found that the progression of the proportion of $f(x)$ which could be assumed to be associated with epidermoid and oat cell carcinomas could be represented by a purely stochastic process.

33. Although the analysis thus proved to be a long and indirect process it did lead to the conclusion that if the deaths could be properly classified the results supported the hypothesis that the lung cancer incidence was associated with the quantity of cigarettes smoked. The stochastic model which describes the process is a "backward" type, i.e. the individual starts with a "stock" of resistance which is reduced over time on a probability basis according to the quantity of cigarettes smoked. The justification is a numerical agreement with observed facts and a common model for both male and female lives.

34. The model so far as I have taken it is incomplete but unless some observed data become available in a suitable form and give separate figures for the two main types of lung cancer there seems little point in refining the model.

35. During the course of this analysis some interesting points fell

to be considered. One of these was the behaviour of the independent mortality rates at the advanced ages. The Registrar General's data is given in quinquennial age groups up to age 85, but thereafter all ages are grouped and it is impossible to determine the true trend beyond this age and thus to decide on the mathematical behaviour of $f(x)$. However, Dr. Benjamin was able to provide some data relating to centenarians and it is not without interest to note that among the 148 male and 1084 female deaths of centenarians from 1956 to 1960 there was only one death (F) attributed to cancer of the lung. It proved impossible to form an opinion regarding the limiting behaviour of $f(x)$.

36. Another aspect of the calculations which provided some interesting thoughts arose from the early calculations of the $\mu = \phi \chi f$ formula. The values of $\phi(T-x)$, i.e. the parameters associated with each year of birth showed a remarkable increase from zero in the early 1800's to a maximum in about 1910 for males and rather later for females. The progression was so regular that I was tempted to seek an explanation on genetic grounds but it soon appeared that no reasonable model could be created to deal with the rates of increase found. This feature seemed to rule out a number of the theories being advanced which sought to identify the increase in lung cancer deaths with factors other than cigarette smoking. It was a satisfactory analytical result to find that the increase could be quantitatively agreed with the proportions of smokers in the generations. Similarly the variations in the numerical values of $\chi(T)$ did tie in with the quantity of tobacco smoked.

37. If this model for lung cancer mortality is correct, then it becomes possible to talk about forecasting the deaths expected in the future from this cause. Once the ϕ, χ, f factors are available the death rates in future years can be calculated but only by making assumptions about the smoking habits of future generations or about the discovery and elimination of the harmful constituents of tobacco. Whether similar models can be found for other causes of death is not known. From my earlier work on the statistical distributions of deaths by causes it would not seem unreasonable to apply the $\phi \chi f$ technique and I would expect the resulting "pure" mortality curves to be logistic in form and capable of representation by stochastic processes. It is conceivable, though I admit unlikely, that physical features will be found to describe the processes but the effort might be worth while. In any case extrapolation based on the

separate cause of death analyses would seem to offer a more scientific basis of forecasting than a purely arithmetical method.

38. The $\phi\chi f$ technique can be looked upon as a crude separation into "nature" and "nurture" since the ϕ parameter is associated with year of birth and the χ parameter with year passed through. But although I have made some limited experiments with other causes of death these have not led to any suggestions that the concept is useful.

39. As a rather different type of analysis I have done some work on the mortality of mice by causes. The idea came after reading an article by Lindop and Rotblat (1961) on their experiments in which series of mice were exposed to different doses of radiation and records kept of their age at death and cause thereof. The age distribution of deaths by causes showed marked changes according to the dosage received but the statistical uncertainty arising from the limited numbers and the size of the "unknown cause" groups were too large for useful conclusions to be drawn.

40. There are a number of interesting features of mortality tables based upon the over-simplifying assumption that causes of death operate independently but this is hardly the occasion to extend this paper. Clearly to move from the assumption that a group of lives is homogeneous to an assumption of heterogeneity must give rise to assumptions as to the form of the heterogeneity. Equally to move from a deterministic to a stochastic model will complicate the analysis still further but without these extensions the study of mortality must remain largely descriptive statistics. So soon as these extensions are introduced the study of mortality becomes the scientific study of living processes.

The following bibliography is a shortened one appropriate to the subject matter of this paper and as such is a necessarily biassed selection of the literature. Beard (1959, 1964) gives a more extended series relevant to this paper, but a more systematic collation of relevant papers will be found in Strehler (1962).

References

BEARD, R. E. (1950) *Proc. Centenary Assembly Inst. Act.* **2,** 89.

BEARD, R. E. (1951a) *J. Inst. Actuaries* **77,** 382.

BEARD, R. E. (1951b) *J. Inst. Actuaries* **77,** 394.

BEARD, R. E. (1952) *J. Inst. Actuaries* **78,** 341.

BEARD, R. E. (1959) *Ciba Fdn Colloq. Ageing*, edited by Wolstenholme and O'Connor, **5,** 302, Appendix, J. & A. Churchill, London.

BEARD, R. E. (1960/1961a) *Trans. Assur. med. Soc.* p. 17.

BEARD, R. E. (1961b) *International Population Conference*, **1,** 611.

BEARD, R. E. (1963) *Proc. R. Soc.* B, **159,** 56.

BEARD, R. E. (1964) *Int. Congr. Actuaries* **3,** 463.

CHIANG, C. L. (1960) *Proc. Berkeley Symp. math. Statist. Probab.*

DERRICK, V. P. A. (1927) *J. Inst. Actuaries* **58,** 117.

GOMPERTZ, B. (1825) *Phil. Trans. R. Soc.* **115,** 513.

KREYBERG, L. (1962) *Histological Lung Cancer Types*, Norwegian University Press, Oslo.

LINDOP, P. and ROTBLAT, J. (1961) *Proc. R. Soc.* B, **154,** 332.

MAKEHAM, W. M. (1867) *J. Inst. Actuaries* **13,** 325.

OGBORN, M. E. (1953) *J. Inst. Actuaries* **79,** 170.

PERKS, W. (1932) *J. Inst. Actuaries* **63,** 12.

PEARSON, K. (1897) *The Chances of Death and other Studies*, Arnold.

PHILLIPS, W. (1954) *J. Inst. Actuaries* **80,** 289.

PRAWITZ, H. (1954) *Svenska Aktuarieforeningen Femtio Av.*

REGISTRAR GENERAL (1958) *Statist. Rev.*

STREHLER, B. L. (1962) *Time, Cells and Aging*, Academic Press, London and New York.

ON THE SCALE OF MORTALITY

W. BRASS

London School of Hygiene & Tropical Medicine, University of London

Introduction

Mortality rates by age have characteristic features which occur in all populations, large enough and observed for sufficiently long periods for erratic fluctuations to be absorbed. The similarities of pattern stimulate a search for simple methods of describing the relationships between mortalities in different countries or at different periods in the same country. We present in this paper a system for describing such relationships by the use of mathematical functions, whereby the mortality rates in a given population are defined by the specification of only two measurements or parameters. By this system sets of mortality patterns (or life tables which are the expression of these patterns in a particular form) are generated. Reference sets of this kind have conventionally been called "models" in demography although the term is unfortunate because of confusion with its rather different meaning in the simulation of processes.

Life-table models or reference sets can be used for a number of purposes. Their most notable application has been for the graduation, adjustment and extension of the limited and defective data from developing countries. The system described here has been widely used in this way (Brass *et al.*, 1968), although no thorough account of its characteristics has been published. The advantage of a simple model, which yet reproduces the main features of the situation, in the analysis of unsatisfactory records is that estimates can be made from a combination of only the more reliable observations. Rather similar conditions hold in the projection of past trends into the future, even for populations with accurate and detailed demographic statistics, and the model has also been applied to the problem (Brass, 1969).

The simplicity of the system for describing relations among mortality patterns suggests that it depends on fundamental properties of the variation in death rates with age. Our main purpose is to investigate this possibility with the aim of gaining new insights into the nature of the variation and providing a meaningful scale for its measurement. To this end we give a detailed account of the model life-table system and examine how closely it represents observations for a variety of populations. An attempt is made to interpret the form of the mathematical relationship which is the basis of the system and some of the implications are pointed out. The applications of the models as "reference-distributions" for description, graduation, adjustment and estimation (which are largely independent of any interpretation) are not dealt with here.

Models of Mortality Patterns

The consistent features in mortality patterns have long been recognized and there have been many attempts to construct mathematical functions of age which would describe the measures, going back to the work of Gompertz (1825). In the main these exercises were confined to death rates at later ages, beyond the period in childhood where minimum levels are reached following the high mortality of infancy. They were mainly based on elaborations of exponential functions. A rather different approach was adopted by others who tried to analyse the "curve of deaths", i.e. the proportional numbers dying at each age from a group of births. For example, Pearson (1948) developed a method for expressing the curve by the combination of three independent Normal distributions covering different periods of life. A useful brief review of these various approaches is given in Benjamin (1964).

More recently there has been a shift in emphasis, dictated by the need for reference-sets of life tables as an aid in the analysis of data from developing countries. Such "reference-sets" have been constructed essentially as averages, over groups of populations, of recorded mortality rates. Various procedures for averaging and translating the results into a systematic grid of life tables over the required range have been devised, mainly by the application of statistical regression techniques. The underlying assumption is that mortality patterns are sufficiently regular for representation by life tables with very limited modes of variation to be useful; the form of the relationship, with age or among the members of the set, is not explicitly brought out. The pioneering sets of model life tables are those of the United Nations (1955); for each sex at a given level of mortality there is one life table, i.e. there is only one dimension of variation (or one parameter). Coale and Demeny (1966) modified and extended the United Nations' system in the selection of basic records and techniques of calculation but primarily by constructing four Regional sets of tables (male and female), each based on groups of populations whose mortality patterns showed distinctive features in common.

The additional variation provided by the Coale–Demeny system made it possible to match recorded life tables more satisfactorily than with the United Nations' models but deviations and anomalies still remain. The theoretical work of Ledermann and Breas (1959) provided valuable guidance on the number of dimensions of variation (parameters) required for a mortality model system to represent closely the known measurements. By a factor analysis of age–specific death rates in a range of populations they showed that two factors (apart from sex) accounted for a substantial part of the variability; two other factors had also an appreciable influence at early and late ages respectively. Procedures for modifying the United Nations models to allow for these findings have been suggested (1962).

Ledermann's studies suggest that mortalities by age in different populations might be approximately related to each other by a function containing as few as two unknown parameters but provide no clues about how such a function could be constructed. In contrast to the long history of attempts to describe death rates by mathematical functions of age the problem of relating mortalities in different populations to each other by such means has been neglected. There appears to be only one context in which the attempt has been made (and somewhat indirectly), namely in the forecasting of future mortality from generation rates.

If trends in mortality in a population are examined the proportional changes in specific death rates over a limited time period do not differ greatly with age in most of the range. This observation was the basis of the classic work by Kermack *et al.* (1934) on generation mortality projections. If $\mu(x)$ is written for the specific death rate at the exact age x (usually called the force of mortality and more convenient for analytic work than the conventional rates for age intervals) the approximate relationship of change becomes $\mu_1(x) = C\mu_2(x)$, where the indices 1 and 2 refer to two life tables at different periods and C is a constant. This is the same as $l_1'(x)/l_1(x) = Cl_2'(x)/l_2(x)$, where the $l(x)$ are the life-table survivors to age x and the dashes denote the differential coefficients. The equation implies further that $\log_e l_1(x) = C \log_e l_2(x)$, where $\log_e$ denotes the natural logarithm, which is usually the most convenient form of presentation. It should be noted that $l_1(x)$ and $l_2(x)$ are both unity and their logarithms zero when x is zero. If a relationship holds between life tables in one population over a long period it seems reasonable that it should also describe mortality patterns in populations at different stages of development.

The Logit System

As an aid in the construction of model life tables by sex the United Nations demographers calculated age schedules at four levels of mortality. These were straightforward averages of probabilities of dying by age group in published records for countries by four intervals of life expectation. The schedules, which are shown in Table 1, form a convenient basis for a preliminary assessment of relationships. It can be seen that the ratios of probabilities of dying in any two schedules are not constant with age but follow a more complicated course, in particular moving closer to unity for older people. For example, the probability of dying in the age group 1–4 years is about 16 times higher in schedule D than in schedule A but the corresponding multiplier at 75–79 years is less than $1\frac{1}{2}$. This suggests the use of a system in which death-rate differences among populations at early years of life are taken as proportional not to the life-table survivors $l(x)$ but to the probability of dying $1 - l(x)$ while the previous relationship is retained at late years. A simple equation of this kind can be derived from the logarithm of $(1 - l(x))/l(x)$. If this is differentiated to give the force of mortality at age x, the relation assumed between two life tables becomes:

$$\frac{l_1'(x)}{l_1(x)(1 - l_1(x))} = C\frac{l_2'(x)}{l_2(x)(1 - l_2(x))}$$

or

$$\frac{\mu_1(x)}{(1 - l_1(x))} = C\frac{\mu_2(x)}{(1 - l_2(x))}.$$

TABLE 1. United Nations average mortality schedules; proportions dying per 1000 by age group (both sexes)

Age group (years)	A	B	C	D
Under 1	37·57	73·51	125·16	199·34
1–4	9·32	28·04	68·78	149·55
5–9	4·62	10·71	19·29	44·70
10–14	3·83	8·25	13·48	28·18
15–19	6·61	14·12	21·81	38·79
20–24	9·40	19·64	29·85	51·11
25–29	10·29	20·81	30·76	54·60
30–34	11·50	22·37	33·05	59·78
35–39	14·19	25·88	37·41	67·11
40–44	19·33	31·62	44·27	77·07
45–49	28·44	41·27	54·42	90·54
50–54	42·67	57·05	72·32	111·70
55–59	63·37	80·38	98·99	143·90
60–64	96·48	117·63	142·88	194·77
65–69	148·56	175·71	205·70	266·84
70–74	230·65	264·56	304·47	373·41
75–79	350·18	389·25	433·87	492·18
80–84	505·60	543·90	584·98	633·05
e_0 (years)	67·63	59·50	50·30	36·77

The range of life expectancies in the tables from which the averages were calculated are:
A: 65 years and over; B: 55·0 to 64·9 years; C: 45 to 54·9 years; D: less than 45 years.

At late ages when the $l(x)$ are small and $1 - l(x)$ close to one the equation is approximately as before. When $l(x)$ is close to one at early ages, the factors $\dfrac{1}{1 - l_1(x)}$ and $\dfrac{1}{1 - l_2(x)}$ will tend to offset the difference between $\mu_1(x)$ and $\mu_2(x)$. At middle ages, when the $l(x)$ are not close to one or zero the compensating effect will be smaller. We may then hope that the use of a fixed constant C in the equation will represent observations better than in the similar relation between forces of mortality only. Integration to obtain a formula in the $l(x)$ gives

$$\log_e [(1 - l_1(x))/l_1(x)] = \alpha_0 + \beta_0 \log_e [(1 - l_2(x))/l_2(x)],$$

where α_0 and β_0 are two constants. Note that an extra constant can be added because the logarithms are both equal to minus infinity when x is zero and $l(x)$ equal to one. The logarithm of p/q, where p

F

is a proportion and q is $l - p$ is a function well known in statistics. With the multiplier one half to give $\frac{1}{2} \log_e p/q$ it is called the logit of p and is widely used in the analysis of bio-assays. The analogy of the present application with bio-assay studies will be considered later. The function is tabulated in the Fisher and Yates Statistical Tables. It is convenient, therefore, to write the relation in terms of the logit of $1 - l(x)$, i.e. $\frac{1}{2} \log_e [(1 - l(x))/l(x)]$ which will be denoted by $Y(x)$. The equation is then $Y_1(x) = \alpha_0 + \beta_0 Y_2(x)$. The α_0 value here would be half that of the previous equation for the same life tables but this will not cause confusion since the logit representation will be used throughout the paper. Note that since logit $l(x) = - \text{logit } (1 - l(x))$, the same system results whether we think in terms of proportions dying before or after age x.

TABLE 2. Proportions surviving from birth and corresponding logits for United Nations average mortality schedules

	Both Sexes							
	$l(x)$				logit			
Age (x) (years)	A	B	C	D	A	B	C	D
1	0·9624	0·9625	0·8748	0·8007	−1·6216	−1·2670	−0·9722	−0·6952
5	0·9535	0·9005	0·8147	0·6809	−1·5099	−1·1015	−0·7403	−0·3790
20	0·9392	0·8710	0·7710	0·6076	−1·3684	−0·9551	−0·6070	−0·2187
30	0·9208	0·8362	0·7250	0·5451	−1·2264	−0·8150	−0·4846	−0·0904
40	0·8973	0·7963	0·6748	0·4781	−1·0836	−0·6816	−0·3650	0·0438
50	0·8549	0·7393	0·6098	0·4013	−0·8868	−0·5212	−0·2233	0·2000
60	0·7666	0·6411	0·5097	0·3052	−0·5945	−0·2900	−0·0195	0·4113
65	0·6926	0·5657	0·4369	0·2458	−0·4062	−0·1316	0·1269	0·5607
70	0·5897	0·4663	0·3470	0·1802	−0·1814	0·0676	0·3161	0·7576
75	0·4537	0·3429	0·2414	0·1129	0·0928	0·3252	0·5726	1·0308
80	0·2948	0·2094	0·1366	0·0573	0·4360	0·6642	0·9218	1·4000

In Table 2 are shown the life-table survivors $l(x)$ and the corresponding logits for the United Nations mortality schedules. Only selected values are given, instead of at five-year intervals of x, since the logits change slowly with age where mortality is relatively low in childhood and early adult years; the presentation of the full results would extend the table without adding anything significant to the comparisons.

The point brought out by the values in the table is that the rather complex relations between the $l(x)$ ratios of the different mortality schedules are transformed by the logits to a much more obvous structure. Thus on the $l(x)$ scale the differences between any pair of schedules, either relatively or absolutely, show no simple age pattern. On the other hand the differences on the logit scale only diverge moderately from a constant level. This is better seen in Table 3 which shows logit differences for adjoining schedules.

TABLE 3. Logit differences for United Nations average mortality schedules

Age x	B–A	C–B	D–C	Age x	B–A	C–B	D–C
1	0·3546	0·2948	0·2770	60	0·3045	0·2705	0·4308
5	0·4084	0·3612	0·3613	65	0·2746	0·2585	0·4338
20	0·4133	0·3481	0·3883	70	0·2490	0·2485	0·4415
30	0·4114	0·3304	0·3942	75	0·2324	0·2474	0·4582
40	0·4020	0·3166	0·4088	80	0·2282	0·2576	0·4782
50	0·3656	0·2979	0·4233				

These differences change slowly and consistently with age although it is interesting to note that the movement for D–C is in the opposite direction to those of the other two sets. In fact the logit differences D–B are almost constant over all ages. There are fluctuations in the trend of differences but these show no systematic pattern except at age one. Here the logits have too small a spread over the range of mortality levels to fit well with the general pattern. The point will be discussed more fully later. It is clear that with this exception the relations between the United Nations average mortality schedules can be described quite well by straight lines on the logit scale.

The Standard Life-Table Base

We are primarily concerned here with the relations between the mortalities of different populations and not the construction of an absolute, unique set of reference life tables (models). In any particular application the choice of a life table to serve as a basic standard pattern can be determined by the aims and the information available. Thus for an investigation of changes in mortality over time in a population the best base would be one of the life tables under study. Nevertheless for many purposes it is convenient to use a standard mortality schedule to which all others can be related. Among the most important applications of reference sets of life tables is the reconstruction of measures for developing territories, where there is little evidence on which to base a decision that some particular detailed pattern of mortality is more likely to be a good representation than others.

In such circumstances, the standard life table must be some kind of average. If two life tables are each to have a straight line relationship to a third on the logit scale then they must also be linear in terms of each other. Any one of a set of life tables thus inter-related could be taken as a standard. In practice, because of deviations from exact linearity, this is not strictly true and some will be better representations of the average pattern than others. A general purpose standard life table has been constructed based mainly on the United Nations B schedule of mortality. In order to move the level of death rates closer to the "central" interval of the range observed in different populations 0.5 was added to the logits of the survivorship proportions of the B schedules. This is equivalent on the logit scale to altering α_0 by a constant, but leaving β_0 unchanged. The more obvious procedure of starting from the United Nations C schedule which is at about the required level of mortality was rejected because the straight line "slope" of the C death rates is not near average, i.e. β_0 values based on this standard would usually be positive. Adjustments were then made to the measures at one year and 65 years and above to make the generated system a better average representation for published life tables, particularly for moderate and high mortalities. The adjustments were made empirically from comparisons with the United Nations mortality schedules and Regional sets of life tables (see below). The size of the modifications to the B schedule logits can be seen in Table 6. Less attention was paid to the course of mortality in countries with low death rates since it will usually be possible to calculate special standards in applications to such data. By these methods a standard life table was constructed to give survivorship proportions at one year, five years and thereafter at five year intervals to 80. For some purposes, measures at finer intervals and beyond 80 years may be required. The standard has been extended to values at single years of age to 50 and at $2\frac{1}{2}$-year intervals to zero at 100. Death rates at ages beyond 80 years were arrived at by the examination of published life tables. In view of the deficiencies in the accuracy of the statistics for this period of life, no great weight can be put on the resulting measures. Values within the standard five year intervals were obtained by interpolation in the logits. The life-table survivorship proportions of the standard and the corresponding logits are shown in Table 4.

TABLE 4. Standard life table measures

Age (x) (years)	$l(x)$	Logit	Age (x) (years)	$l(x)$	Logit	Age (x) (years)	$l(x)$	Logit
0	1·0000	$-\infty$	25	0·6826	$-0·3829$	50	0·5106	$-0·0212$
1	0·8499	$-0·8670$	26	0·6764	$-0·3686$	52½	0·4857	0·0286
2	0·8070	$-0·7152$	27	0·6703	$-0·3549$	55	0·4585	0·0832
3	0·7876	$-0·6552$	28	0·6643	$-0·3413$	57½	0·4291	0·1428
4	0·7762	$-0·6219$	29	0·6584	$-0·3280$	60	0·3965	0·2100
5	0·7691	$-0·6015$	30	0·6525	$-0·3150$	62½	0·3602	0·2873
6	0·7642	$-0·5879$	31	0·6466	$-0·3020$	65	0·3210	0·3746
7	0·7601	$-0·5766$	32	0·6405	$-0·2889$	67½	0·2801	0·4720
8	0·7564	$-0·5666$	33	0·6345	$-0·2759$	70	0·2380	0·5818
9	0·7532	$-0·5578$	34	0·6284	$-0·2627$	72½	0·1945	0·7105
10	0·7502	$-0·5498$	35	0·6223	$-0·2496$	75	0·1500	0·8673
11	0·7477	$-0·5431$	36	0·6160	$-0·2364$	77½	0·1090	1·0505
12	0·7452	$-0·5365$	37	0·6097	$-0·2230$	80	0·0760	1·2490
13	0·7425	$-0·5296$	38	0·6032	$-0·2094$	82½	0·0490	1·4828
14	0·7396	$-0·5220$	39	0·5966	$-0·1956$	85	0·0290	1·7555
15	0·7362	$-0·5131$	40	0·5898	$-0·1817$	87½	0·0155	2·0760
16	0·7328	$-0·5043$	41	0·5830	$-0·1676$	90	0·0070	2·4774
17	0·7287	$-0·4941$	42	0·5759	$-0·1530$	92½	0·0030	2·9031
18	0·7241	$-0·4824$	43	0·5686	$-0·1381$	95	0·0010	3·4534
19	0·7188	$-0·4694$	44	0·5612	$-0·1229$	97½	0·0001	4·6046
20	0·7130	$-0·4551$	45	0·5535	$-0·1073$	100	0·0000	∞
21	0·7069	$-0·4401$	46	0·5454	$-0·0911$			
22	0·7005	$-0·4248$	47	0·5371	$-0·0743$			
23	0·6943	$-0·4103$	48	0·5285	$-0·0572$			
24	0·6884	$-0·3963$	49	0·5197	$-0·0395$			

Characteristics of Life Tables of the System

If the standard logits are symbolized by $Y_s(x)$, where x is age, the equation relating other schedules of mortality to this function is $Y(x) = \alpha + \beta Y_s(x)$, where α and β are constants which vary among life tables. $Y_s(x)$ is zero when $l_s(x)$ is 0·5, i.e. at the age (here 51 years) to which half the births survive. Since $Y(x)$ is then equal to α this parameter can be regarded, in a sense, as measuring the level of mortality although, since the pattern of specific death rates with age varies with β, the term "level" is not fully defined. In this paper the phrase "level of mortality" will be used in a general way. More specific definition will be given by reference to values of α and β. A positive value of α gives an $l(x)$ survivorship of less than 0·5 at age 51 years. If β is also equal to unity $Y(x) - Y_s(x)$ has the value α at all ages, and, consequently, the differences between $l(x)$ and $l_s(x)$ are in the same direction throughout. The generated life table then has a higher mortality than the standard. If β is greater than one, however, the difference between $Y(x)$ and $Y_s(x)$ will be less than α at ages below 51 years. For example, if α was 0·18 and β was 1·3, $l(x)$ would be almost exactly equal to $l_s(x)$ at age five years but 0·411 at 51 years compared with the standard 0·5. A β greater than one means that with increasing age the survivorship ratios of the life table fall more rapidly than those for a population with the α, but β equal to one; the opposite holds for β less than one. It is convenient, therefore, to call β the "slope" of mortality.

In order to give a clearer conception of the implications of α and β life tables have been computed for various values of the parameters. The $l(x)$ survivorship proportions, probabilities of dying in age groups, and expectations of life, for a selection of these are shown in Table 5. The limits adopted for β cover approximately the range observed for recorded mortality schedules in order to illustrate the characteristics of variations in the parameter. The effects of extreme variations in β can be seen by comparing, say, the life tables for β equal to 0·6, $\alpha = -1\cdot00$ and β equal to 1·6, $\alpha = -0\cdot50$. In both rather over 93 per cent of the population survive to age five years (93·8 per cent and 94·9 per cent). On the other hand, the $l(x)$ measures are 78·6 per cent and 29·7 per cent respectively at 70 years of age.

Comparisons with Average Mortality Schedules

In comparing empirical life tables with the logit reference system it is often convenient to examine $Y(x) - Y_s(x)$ which will be denoted by $D(x)$. The logit equation can be written as $D(x) = Y(x) - Y_s(x) = \alpha + (\beta - 1)Y_s(x)$. It is useful to consider $D(x)$ because $(\beta - 1)$ is usually quite close to zero; deviations from the standard are thus exhibited as variations about a constant or slowly changing level. They can, therefore, be easily appreciated both numerically and graphically.

It is now appropriate to return to the United Nations mortality

TABLE 5. Survivors from 10,000 births (*l*), expectation of life (*e*) and probability of dying before next stated age (*q*) in selected logit model life tables

$\beta = 0 \cdot 6$

Age (years)	$\alpha = 0 \cdot 5$			$\alpha = 0$			$\alpha = -0 \cdot 5$			$\alpha = -1 \cdot 0$		
	l	*q*	*e*	*l*	*q*	*e*	*l*	*q*	*e*	*l*	*q*	*e*
0	10,000	0·4899	24·7	10,000	0·2611	43·1	10,000	0·1150	61·7	10,000	0·0456	75·8
1	5,101	0·1553	47·0	7,389	0·0892	57·2	8,850	0·0413	68·6	9,544	0·0098	78·4
5	4,309	0·0352	51·4	6,730	0·0205	58·7	8,484	0·0096	67·5	9,383	0·0039	75·7
10	4,158	0·0256	48·2	6,592	0·0151	54·8	8,402	0·0071	63·1	9,346	0·0029	71·0
15	4,051	0·0412	44·4	6,493	0·0247	50·6	8,342	0·0118	58·6	9,319	0·0049	66·2
20	3,884	0·0524	41·2	6,332	0·0321	46·9	8,243	0·0156	54·2	9,273	0·0065	61·5
25	3,681	0·0509	38·3	6,129	0·0318	43·3	8,115	0·0157	50·1	9,212	0·0066	56·9
30	3,493	0·0504	35·2	5,934	0·0321	39·7	7,987	0·0162	45·8	9,151	0·0069	52·3
35	3,317	0·0538	32·0	5,743	0·0350	35·9	7,858	0·0179	41·5	9,088	0·0077	47·6
40	3,139	0·0600	28·6	5,543	0·0398	32·1	7,717	0·0208	37·3	9,018	0·0091	43·0
45	2,950	0·0714	25·3	5,322	0·0485	28·4	7,556	0·0259	33·0	8,937	0·0115	38·4
50	2,740	0·0883	22·1	5,064	0·0618	24·7	7,360	0·0340	28·8	8,834	0·0153	33·8
55	2,498	0·1098	19·0	4,751	0·0795	21·1	7,110	0·0454	24·7	8,699	0·0209	29·3
60	2,224	0·1451	16·0	4,373	0·1094	17·7	6,787	0·0655	20·8	8,517	0·0314	24·8
65	1,901	0·1861	13·3	3,895	0·1470	14·6	6,342	0·0936	17·1	8,250	0·0471	20·6
70	1,547	0·2567	10·8	3,322	0·2143	11·7	5,749	0·1480	13·6	7,861	0·0804	16·4
75	1,150	0·3400	8·6	2,610	0·3003	9·2	4,898	0·2286	10·5	7,230	0·1386	12·7
80	759	0·4361	6·8	1,826	0·4061	7·1	3,778	0·3423	7·9	6,227	0·2399	9·3
85	428	0·5678	5·1	1,085	0·5513	5·3	2,485	0·5087	5·6	4,734	0·4205	6·4
90	185	1·0000	3·7	487	1·0000	3·8	1,221	1·0000	3·9	2,743	1·0000	4·2

TABLE 5 (continued)

$\beta = 1 \cdot 0$

Age (years)	α = 0·5			α = 0			α = −0·5			α = −1·0		
	l	q	e	l	q	e	l	q	e	l	q	e
0	10,000	0·3244	26·9	10,000	0·1501	43·4	10,000	0·0610	58·9	10,000	0·0233	70·7
1	6,756	0·1850	38·5	8,499	0·0951	50·0	9,390	0·0409	61·7	9,767	0·0161	71·4
5	5,506	0·0467	43·0	7,691	0·0246	51·1	9,005	0·0107	60·3	9,610	0·0042	68·6
10	5,249	0·0349	40·0	7,502	0·0187	47·4	8,909	0·0082	55·9	9,569	0·0033	63·8
15	5,066	0·0574	36·3	7,362	0·0315	43·2	8,835	0·0142	51·4	9,538	0·0057	59·0
20	4,775	0·0750	33·4	7,130	0·0426	39·5	8,710	0·0196	47·1	9,483	0·0080	54·4
25	4,417	0·0750	30·9	6,826	0·0441	36·2	8,539	0·0208	43·0	9,408	0·0085	49·8
30	4,086	0·0763	28·2	6,525	0·0463	32·7	8,362	0·0224	38·8	9,328	0·0093	45·2
35	3,774	0·0833	25·3	6,223	0·0522	29·2	8,175	0·0259	34·7	9,241	0·0110	40·6
40	3,460	0·0947	22·4	5,898	0·0616	25·7	7,963	0·0315	30·5	9,140	0·0136	36·0
45	3,132	0·1144	19·5	5,535	0·0775	22·2	7,712	0·0413	26·4	9,016	0·0182	31·5
50	2,774	0·1437	16·7	5,106	0·1020	18·9	7,393	0·0571	22·5	8,852	0·0260	27·0
55	2,375	0·1805	14·0	4,585	0·1352	15·7	6,971	0·0804	18·7	8,622	0·0383	22·7
60	1,947	0·2389	11·6	3,965	0·1904	12·8	6,410	0·1227	15·1	8,292	0·0624	18·5
65	1,482	0·3044	9·4	3,210	0·2586	10·2	5,624	0·1835	11·9	7,774	0·1026	14·5
70	1,031	0·4085	7·4	2,380	0·3698	7·9	4,592	0·2940	9·0	6,977	0·1888	10·9
75	610	0·5182	5·8	1,500	0·4933	6·1	3,242	0·4363	6·7	5,660	0·3321	7·8
80	294	0·6299	4·6	760	0·6184	4·7	1,827	0·5891	4·9	3,780	0·5217	5·5
85	109	0·7617	3·5	290	0·7586	3·5	751	0·7496	3·6	1,808	0·7261	3·8
90	26	1·0000	2·7	70	1·0000	2·7	188	1·0000	2·7	495	1·0000	2·8

TABLE 5 (continued)

$\beta = 1\cdot6$

Age (years)	$\alpha = 0\cdot5$			$\alpha = 0$			$\alpha = -0\cdot5$			$\alpha = -1\cdot0$		
	l	q	e	l	q	e	l	q	e	l	q	e
0	10,000	0·1450	31·0	10,000	0·0587	45·0	10,000	0·0224	57·2	10,000	0·0084	66·5
1	8,550	0·1624	35·1	9,413	0·0728	46·8	9,776	0·0292	57·5	9,916	0·0111	66·1
5	7,161	0·0487	37·7	8,727	0·0224	46·4	9,491	0·0091	55·2	9,806	0·0035	62·8
10	6,812	0·0382	34·5	8,532	0·0180	42·4	9,405	0·0074	50·7	9,772	0·0028	58·0
15	6,552	0·0659	30·7	8,378	0·0321	38·1	9,335	0·0134	46·0	9,745	0·0052	53·1
20	6,121	0·0915	27·7	8,109	0·0468	34·3	9,210	0·0201	41·6	9,694	0·0079	48·4
25	5,561	0·0972	25·3	7,730	0·0522	30·8	9,025	0·0231	37·4	9,618	0·0092	43·8
30	5,020	0·1038	22·7	7,326	0·0586	27·4	8,816	0·0268	33·3	9,529	0·0108	39·2
35	4,499	0·1181	20·1	6,897	0·0702	23·9	8,580	0·0334	29·1	9,426	0·0138	34·6
40	3,968	0·1391	17·4	6,413	0·0876	20·6	8,294	0·0437	25·0	9,296	0·0185	30·0
45	3,416	0·1730	14·8	5,851	0·1165	17·3	7,931	0·0617	21·1	9,124	0·0271	25·5
50	2,825	0·2215	12·4	5,170	0·1608	14·2	7,442	0·0921	17·3	8,877	0·0426	21·2
55	2,199	0·2809	10·3	4,338	0·2208	11·5	6,756	0·1397	13·8	8,499	0·0699	17·0
60	1,581	0·3685	8·3	3,380	0·3145	9·1	5,813	0·2250	10·6	7,905	0·1268	13·1
65	999	0·4586	6·7	2,317	0·4196	7·1	4,505	0·3408	8·0	6,903	0·2257	9·6
70	541	0·5855	5·2	1,345	0·5637	5·4	2,970	0·5121	5·8	5,345	0·4100	6·7
75	224	0·7006	4·0	587	0·6925	4·0	1,449	0·6715	4·2	3,153	0·6209	4·6
80	67	0·8018	3·2	180	0·7993	3·2	476	0·7941	3·2	1,195	0·7813	3·3
85	13	0·9023	2·5	36	0·9006	2·5	98	0·8998	2·5	261	0·8982	2·5
90	1	1·0000	2·0	4	1·0000	2·0	10	1·0000	2·0	27	1·0000	2·0

schedules and examine them in terms of the standard life table. The
$D(x)$ values for selected ages are given in Table 6. It is worth noting
that, since each $l(x)$ proportion is derived from the preceding one by
multiplying by the probability of surviving the age interval, large
deviations of an empirical life table from the logit system do not
occur only at isolated ages except possibly at the extremes of life.
Typically they consist of a gradual change in the pattern as the

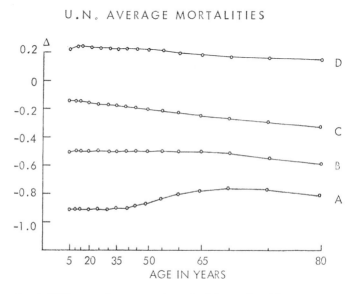

FIG. 1. Differences from general standard in survivorship to ages on
logit scale by mortality level.

specific death rates over an age span diverge from those implied by
the reference standard. It is not essential, therefore, that in comparisons the $l(x)$ proportions should be shown at narrow age
intervals. The $D(x)$ values are plotted against $Y_s(x)$ in Graph 1. It can
be seen from the table and graph that the relations between $D(x)$
and $Y_s(x)$ are quite well represented by straight lines. The deviations
show no consistent features except at one year and perhaps in old
age; the implications of these discrepancies are discussed later.

Although variations and anomalies in mortality patterns are most clearly exhibited on the logit scale it is useful to translate the meaning of such effects in terms of conventional life-table measures. For the purpose it is necessary to select a life table from the reference system for comparison. In effect this is the same as fitting a straight

TABLE 6. Values of $D(x)$ for United Nations mortality schedules

Age (years)	A	B	C	D
1	−0·7546	−0·4000	−0·1052	0·1718
5	−0·9084	−0·5000	−0·1388	0·2225
20	−0·9133	−0·5000	−0·1519	0·2364
30	−0·9114	−0·5000	−0·1696	0·2246
40	−0·9019	−0·5000	−0·1833	0·2255
50	−0·8656	−0·5000	−0·2021	0·2212
60	−0·8045	−0·5000	−0·2295	0·2013
65	−0·7808	−0·5062	−0·2477	0·1861
70	−0·7632	−0·5142	−0·2657	0·1758
75	−0·7745	−0·5421	−0·2947	0·1635
80	−0·8130	−0·5848	−0·3272	0·1510

line to the $l(x)$ values on the logit scale. Similar procedures are required for practical applications of the system for the graduation of observed mortalities which are subject to error. There is no technique which is obviously "right" for carrying out such fitting or graduation. What is required is a method which will give graduated rates close to the true ones, over the range of ages which is important for the purpose considered, when there are no errors in the observations and which will minimize the influence of errors when they are present. The orthodox solution would be to fit a straight line to the observations by the method of least squares, although the theoretical structure of chance error which justifies the technique is unlikely to be relevant. More important is the fact that the method gives much weight to the extreme values (at age one year and in old age). It seems reasonable that they should be given relatively little weight since they fit the system poorly, are subject to large errors of reporting and are less important for the desired applications. It would be possible to devise a weighted least squares procedure which allowed for this but it would be arbitrary and laborious to apply. Since some arbitrariness is inevitable it seems better to take the opportunity to use a technique which is simple in operation.

The procedure adopted is as follows. The observations in order of age are broken into two groups of equal numbers, i.e. the $l(x)$ ratios in the first group are all for ages which are lower than those in the second group. The measure at age one is excluded from the groups because of its erratic relation with the subsequent trend. The mean values of the logits of the $l(x)$ ratios are calculated separately for groups 1 and 2 and also the corresponding means for the standard life table, i.e. those for measures at the same ages. The straight line which joins the two points defined by the mean logits of the observations and standard for groups 1 and 2 respectively is taken as the best fit.

The method is expressed algebraically by summing the logit equation over the two groups so that

$$\sum_1 Y(x) = n\alpha + \beta \sum_1 Y_s(x),$$
$$\sum_2 Y(x) = n\alpha + \beta \sum_2 Y_s(x),$$

where n is the number of observations in each group and $\sum_1$ denotes summation over group 1, etc. Solving for α and β gives the required straight line.

The grouping of the observations for this procedure will depend on the data. If equal age intervals are used the values are closer together on the logit scale in the earlier compared with the later years. This is a desirable property since the dominance of the proportions surviving at the older ages is reduced. The mean values of the two groups lie at the survivorship levels of childhood or early adulthood and towards the end of working life respectively. In fitting straight lines to survivorship ratios in published life tables for an assessment of the features of the logit system the measures at 5-year intervals from 5–80 years inclusive were separated into two equal groups of eight with the division at between 40 and 45 years. The procedure was applied to the United Nations mortality schedules with the results in Table 7.

TABLE 7. Survivors from 1000 births in United Nations mortality schedules observed (o) and fitted (f) by logit model

Age (years)	A o	A f	B o	B f	C o	C f	D o	D f
0	1000	1000	1000	1000	1000	1000	1000	1000
1	962	975	927	938	875	875	801	774
5	953	956	901	900	815	814	681	673
10	949	950	891	890	799	800	650	651
15	945	946	884	883	788	789	632	635
20	939	939	871	871	771	771	608	609
25	930	930	854	854	748	748	577	576
30	921	919	836	837	725	725	545	544
35	910	908	817	818	701	701	513	513
40	897	894	796	798	675	674	478	481
45	880	877	771	773	645	644	441	446
50	855	855	739	743	610	608	401	406
55	818	824	697	702	566	564	356	359
60	767	779	641	647	510	508	305	305
65	693	709	566	571	437	435	246	243
70	590	605	466	470	347	347	180	178
75	454	448	343	337	241	242	113	112
80	295	257	209	194	137	139	57	57
α	−0·8631		−0·5027		−0·2023		0·2112	
β	1·1167		0·9944		0·8913		0·9525	

The observed and fitted survivorship values are in satisfactory agreement except at age one year and, for schedule A, at very late ages. Similar discrepancies in pattern appear also in comparisons made later. They raise issues which may be important in some applications but need only be examined briefly for the present purposes. At late ages, the observed rates for nearly all moderate to high mortality populations are of doubtful accuracy; reports of ages towards the upper limit of life, both at censuses and death registration, are subject to large errors. It might, therefore, have been better in the construction of the standard life table to rely more heavily on the reported pattern of mortality at high ages in the countries with low death rates. If this had been done the agreement of the fitted with observed measures would have been improved for schedule A. Correspondingly the fit at late ages would have been worse in schedules C and D but because of the low proportions surviving the effect would have been less marked on the conventional scale.

The discrepancies at one year, and to a lesser extent, at five years, can be reduced if very early deaths due to endogenous causes are classed with foetal mortality and omitted from the life tables. The trends in the rates for these early deaths with improved health conditions have been much more similar to the movements for still-births than to those for other infant deaths. In principle it is easy to make corrections which allow for the omission of endogenous child mortality but in practice the procedure is cumbersome and will not be introduced here. We will be concerned with the broad features of the system rather than detailed comparisons at particular ages.

Differentials by Sex

It has been shown that average mortality schedules at different levels are reasonably described by the logit system based on a fixed standard. The next question to consider is the adequacy of the system either with the same standard or specially constructed standards for sub-groups of mortality schedules. The divisions by sex are the first which must be examined. The deviations between male and female mortality patterns are most clearly illustrated by the differences between logits of the life-table survivorship proportions at corresponding ages. These differences at selected ages for the United Nations mortality schedules are given in Table 8.

The male logits are larger than the female in each average schedule, indicating consistently poorer survival. The differences increase moderately at ages beyond 40 years but also tend to be larger, except in countries with low death rates, at earlier years. Thus the female advantage in youth and later ages is reversed, or at least not added to, during the reproductive period, presumably because of the

TABLE 8. Differences between logits of $l(x)$ for United Nations mortality tables by sex (male minus female)

Age (years)	A	B	C	D
1	0·1296	0·1183	0·0887	0·0663
5	0·1226	0·0957	0·0644	0·0398
20	0·1314	0·0819	0·0482	0·0212
30	0·1349	0·0768	0·0462	0·0077
40	0·1249	0·0732	0·0474	0·0003
50	0·1331	0·0906	0·0741	0·0213
60	0·1676	0·1237	0·1207	0·0581
65	0·1841	0·1411	0·1458	0·0744
70	0·1930	0·1555	0·1686	0·0905
75	0·1943	0·1681	0·1903	0·1035
80	0·1978	0·1849	0·2151	0·1225

influence of child-bearing. Since the differences are not consistently linear on the logit scale and reflect a similar although not the same divergence for the various mortality schedules, some advantage would be gained by the use of standard life tables for each sex rather than one in common. On the other hand, it seems that the gain would be small. Male and female standards have been constructed by adjustment of the B mortality schedule analogously to the procedure for the combined life table. They are shown in Table 9. To examine the improvement in fit which results from the use of separate standards the United Nations average male mortality schedules

TABLE 9. Standard life table measures for males and females

Age (x) (years)	Males		Females	
	$l(x)$	logit	$l(x)$	logit
0	1·0000	$-\infty$	1·0000	$-\infty$
1	0·8348	$-0·8100$	0·8639	$-0·9240$
5	0·7571	$-0·5684$	0·7806	$-0·6346$
10	0·7395	$-0·5217$	0·7605	$-0·5777$
20	0·7056	$-0·4371$	0·7204	$-0·4732$
30	0·6489	$-0·3071$	0·6561	$-0·3230$
* 40 and over	As in Table 4 for both sexes			

* It was possible by linear transformation of the logits to construct standards which to a sufficiently good approximation were the same for both sexes at 40 years of age and over.

TABLE 10. Survivors from 1000 births in United Nations male mortality schedules observed (o) and fitted with general (f_g) and male (f_m) standards

Age (yrs.)	A			B			C			D		
	o	f_g	f_m	o	f_g	f_m	o	f_g	f_m	o	f_g	f_m
1	958	972	970	919	935	931	865	875	868	790	775	764
5	948	951	949	892	894	891	805	810	806	673	672	666
10	943	945	944	882	883	881	790	794	791	643	649	645
20	932	932	932	862	861	862	763	763	763	603	606	605
30	911	909	910	826	825	827	716	712	715	543	538	541
40	886	881	884	785	783	787	665	658	663	478	473	479
50	839	837	839	722	723	726	593	587	591	396	396	400
60	738	751	753	614	621	622	480	479	481	293	294	295
70	544	564	562	429	436	434	309	313	311	167	167	166
80	254	220	213	179	167	163	112	114	111	51	51	50

have been fitted both with the general and the male standard. The comparisons are shown in Table 10. The agreement between the observed and the fitted measures is appreciably improved by the use of the male standard f_m for medium mortality schedules (B and C) as is to be expected because of the method of construction. The fit with the general standard f_g is nevertheless quite reasonable. At the more extreme mortality levels (A and D) where agreement with the f_g values is rather poorer the measures based on the male standard f_m are little or no better. It can be concluded that the use of the general standard gives results for the sexes separately which are little worse than those for the combined mortality schedules; the adoption of separate standards by sex would improve the detailed fit of the logit system in a limited range of mortality levels but the overall gain for broad descriptive purposes would be slight.

Comparisons with Coale–Demeny Model Life Tables

The Coale–Demeny tables which were described in the introduction provide convenient sets of "average" mortality patterns for sub-groups (here, the "Regions" of the system). The schedules are not now "averages" in a straightforward sense but since they are calculated from life tables for small groups of countries, exhibiting closely similar patterns, they can be taken as equivalent for the present purpose. It should be noted, however, that the extreme schedules in the Regional system are extrapolations to a greater or

TABLE 11. Values of $D(x)$ for Regional mortality schedules

Age (years)	High mortality				Medium mortality				Low mortality			
	North	South	East	West	North	South	East	West	North	South	East	West
1	0·3558	0·2918	0·5228	0·4458	0·0175	0·0713	0·2225	0·0044	−0·9017	−0·7685	−0·7775	−0·7721
5	0·4668	0·4551	0·4973	0·4772	0·0830	0·1597	0·169C	−0·0119	−1·0310	−0·9636	−0·9716	−0·9285
20	0·5331	0·4535	0·4713	0·4889	0·1276	0·1386	0·1345	−0·0160	−1·0093	−1·0702	−1·0247	−0·9468
30	0·5192	0·4302	0·4342	0·4897	0·1046	0·1012	0·0905	−0·0320	−0·9799	−1·1648	−1·0602	−0·9550
40	0·5297	0·4115	0·4191	0·5180	0·0969	0·0693	0·0646	−0·0296	−0·9663	−1·2271	−1·0735	−0·9477
50	0·5383	0·3797	0·4011	0·5438	0·0802	0·0259	0·0356	−0·0345	−0·9517	−1·2538	−1·0431	−0·9085
60	0·5364	0·3383	0·3805	0·5673	0·0410	0·0312	−0·0019	−0·0494	−0·9319	−1·2339	−0·9603	−0·8394
65	0·5426	0·3310	0·3797	0·5896	0·0149	−0·0571	−0·0136	−0·0604	−0·9299	−1·2272	−0·9215	−0·8092
70	0·5730	0·3477	0·4041	0·6228	−0·0065	−0·0731	−0·0162	−0·0733	−0·9293	−1·2208	−0·8856	−0·7838
75	0·6428	0·3986	0·4473	0·6699	−0·0308	−0·0807	−0·0195	−0·0990	−0·9606	−1·2206	−0·8718	−0·7877
80	0·7824	0·5255	0·5460	0·7666	−0·0403	−0·0567	−0·0028	−0·1230	−1·0264	−1·2413	−0·8840	−0·8101

less extent. In particular, for all Regions the schedules constructed for very high mortality levels extend well beyond the range of the observed life tables; for certain Regions there is also some stretching at low mortalities. For the comparisons here only schedules reasonably within the range of the observations are taken. With this restriction high, medium and low mortality schedules for each sex were selected from each of the four Regional sets. The corresponding male and female measures were averaged to give combined life tables. The logit differences from the general standard at corresponding ages are shown in Table 11. The roughly linear relationships on the logit scale between the standard and the United Nations average mortality schedules is also apparent for the Regional groups. To some extent the variations among Regional patterns are described by changes in the slope of the relationship, i.e. in the value of β, although not consistently at the different mortality levels. Thus for the West Region, for high and low mortalities the logit differences become more positive with increasing age (i.e. $\beta < 1 \cdot 0$) but at the medium mortality level the trend is reversed ($\beta > 1 \cdot 0$). There are also particular deviations in the Regional schedules in certain parts of the age range, most notably for the North and South at one year and for the South and East at late ages.

The selected Regional mortality schedules have been fitted by the logit system with the general standard. The results are given in Table 12. The characteristics of the agreement for the West survivorship proportions are essentially the same as for the United Nations schedules, discussed above. This is not surprising since the group of published life tables from which the West set was constructed contained by far the largest number of series. The North comparisons have rather similar features, except for the large discrepancy at one year of age and a smaller deviation in the same direction at five years for low and medium mortalities. The agreement of the fitted and observed measures at one year is also poor for the South schedules and for this Regional set, there are also appreciable discrepancies at older ages due to the particularly high death rates recorded at over 70 years. The fitted measures for the East schedules tend to be too high in childhood and low in the middle adult ages (30 to 50 years). In summary, the fitting could clearly be improved for all Regions except the West by the use of separate standards with modifications at very early and late years. The device of eliminating endogenous infant mortality from the life tables

TABLE 12. Survivors from 1000 births for Regional mortality tables (both sexes) observed (o) and fitted (f) (N = North, S = South, E = East, W = West)

Life table			1	5	10	20	30	40	50	60	70	80	α β
	N	o	735	567	512	461	399	333	262	184	90	17	α= 0·5530
		f	684	549	521	470	396	329	257	174	86	23	β= 1·0813
	S	o	760	573	540	501	442	387	328	250	135	28	α= 0·4141
High		f	686	572	548	504	439	380	313	228	129	35	β= 0·9274
mortality	E	o	666	552	525	492	441	383	319	235	122	30	α= 0·4405
		f	683	565	541	496	430	369	302	218	121	37	β= 0·9492
	W	o	699	562	532	483	413	338	260	174	82	17	α= 0·5494
		f	707	568	539	485	406	335	259	171	81	19	β= 1·1402
	N	o	845	738	699	658	604	542	471	377	240	82	α= 0·0691
		f	804	719	699	663	605	547	475	374	235	85	β= 0·8947
	S	o	831	707	683	653	605	556	498	412	266	84	α= 0·0481
Medium		f	788	707	689	655	602	550	484	392	261	107	β= 0·8120
mortality	E	o	784	704	683	655	610	558	493	396	244	76	α= 0·0638
		f	796	712	694	658	602	546	477	380	245	93	β= 0·8593
	W	o	849	773	754	720	661	604	528	420	266	96	α= −0·0422
		f	849	772	755	720	664	606	531	422	266	93	β= 0·9468
	N	o	972	963	959	949	930	909	875	809	667	390	α= −0·9763
		f	978	962	958	949	932	912	881	819	673	335	β= 1·0576
	S	o	964	958	957	955	951	944	928	886	782	496	α= −1·1668
Low		f	978	966	963	957	946	933	915	880	798	566	β= 0·8282
mortality	E	o	964	959	957	951	940	925	894	818	647	325	α= −0·9927
		f	980	964	960	952	936	916	884	822	671	322	β= 1·0939
	W	o	964	955	952	943	927	905	865	779	600	294	α= −0·8943
		f	977	959	954	943	924	900	863	789	618	255	β= 1·1252

would lead to some improvement at age one year but considerable residual discrepancies would remain. It appears, however, that the pattern of mortality at early ages is very variable even among countries which have been allocated to the same Regional set of tables. Thus with virtually the same proportions dead by age five years in the male life tables (163 and 164 from 1000) Denmark in 1901–05 shows 131 dead before one year compared with the England and Wales 1916–20 number of 111. Although in all countries mortality is relatively high in infancy and is reduced to a low level by about the fourth or fifth years of life, the pattern of the fall, particularly in the second year, is far from consistent. There must be some doubts, therefore, about the description of these features by averages without supplementary information. At late years, as already pointed out, the problem of the accuracy of the reported death rates becomes acute. Since mortality is then high the percentage error in reporting need not be large for a considerable distortion of the survivorship proportions to occur.

The South schedules are least well fitted by the use of the general standard. To illustrate the kind of improved agreement which comes from the adoption of a special standard the South schedules of high and low mortality have been fitted by a linear logit system using the selected medium mortality life table as a base. The results are given in Table 13. Although the agreement is better than that

TABLE 13. Survivors from 1000 births for South mortality schedules (both sexes) observed (o) and fitted by special (f_s) and general (f_g) standards

		Age (years)									
		1	5	10	20	30	40	50	60	70	80
High mortality	o	760	573	540	501	442	387	328	250	135	28
	f_s	750	572	540	501	443	387	325	245	132	31
	f_g	686	572	548	504	439	380	313	228	129	35
Low mortality	o	964	958	957	955	951	944	928	886	782	496
	f_s	983	966	961	956	946	935	919	888	801	500
	f_g	978	966	963	957	946	933	915	880	798	566

obtained with the general standard, not all the distortion is removed. In particular some of the features of the low mortality pattern, notably the very reduced death rates between five and forty years are not present in the medium schedule which was taken as the standard. It may be concluded that although sub-groups of life tables will be better described by logit systems based on appropriate special standards rather than the general one, the advantages of such modifications are limited both by variations in the patterns with the level of mortality and doubts about the extent to which individual life tables will conform.

Comparisons with Observed Mortality Schedules of Particular Populations

The preceding examination has been of the relation of the logit system to "averages" of mortality measures for groups of populations. It is to be expected that many observed life tables will have typical patterns which can be fitted with much the same accuracy as the corresponding "average" mortality schedules. There are, however, variants from the average and it does not necessarily follow that these can conveniently be included in the system. Some of these variants are simply the extremes of ranges which were accepted for the calculation of the Regional schedules. Others were not incorporated in the sets of tables from which the average schedules were constructed. In general these latter, excluded life tables are derived from less reliable statistics. Nevertheless, it would be unwise to dismiss as spurious the more extreme mortality patterns they exhibit. In some cases at least there is good reason to accept the broad course of mortality with age which they exhibit as genuine even if there are distortions over parts of the range. Since the countries of the world for which death statistics of good accuracy exist have a restricted spread of geographic, social and economic conditions, the assumption that mortality patterns are the same in other areas has little justification. The logit system with the general standard has been fitted to a number of life tables for individual populations. Two categories were selected. Table 14A compares observed proportions surviving and the corresponding fitted measures for life tables which were included in the groups from which the Regional schedules were constructed. Also shown are survivorship proportions of the Regional mortality schedule which most nearly conforms to the observations, in the sense that the mean absolute deviations are a minimum; interpolation in the Coale–Demeny sets was used where necessary. The first four examples are for European countries which are each reasonably typical of a Regional set; the last two are for the only populations not mainly of European descent included in the records from which Coale and Demeny constructed their system. Similar comparisons are made in Table 14B but for some of the life tables, not used in the Regional set calculations, which show more extreme discrepancies from average mortality patterns. Although there must be some doubt about the detailed accuracy of these life tables, it can plausibly be argued that the broad characteristics of the deviations are genuine.

TABLE 14A. Survivors from 1000 births for selected life tables observed (o), fitted (f) and corresponding regional schedule (f_i) (i = n, s, e, w for North, South, East, West)

Life table		1	5	10	20	30	40	50	60	70	80	α β
Sweden: females, 1959	f	993	986	984	980	972	961	942	899	775	384	$\alpha = -1\cdot36$
	o	987	984	982	979	974	965	943	891	757	447	$\beta = 1\cdot28$
	f_w	986	983	982	979	974	965	944	890	757	450	
Czechoslovakia: males, 1958	f	982	965	961	951	932	907	867	784	588	210	$\alpha = -0\cdot90$
	o	967	961	958	950	934	915	876	769	549	251	$\beta = 1\cdot25$
	f_e	961	956	953	946	931	914	877	781	586	274	
Italy: females, 1901–11	f	810	738	722	691	643	594	532	443	308	136	$\alpha = -0\cdot04$
	o	848	739	721	699	641	592	541	466	317	107	$\beta = 0\cdot77$
	f_s	850	738	716	687	643	597	546	469	321	113	
Norway: females, 1946–50	f	975	957	952	942	924	902	868	801	648	310	$\alpha = -0\cdot91$
	o	966	958	953	942	924	902	865	791	639	353	$\beta = 1\cdot05$
	f_n	966	951	945	935	917	894	859	796	659	386	
Japan: males, 1959	f	976	955	950	937	914	885	839	749	547	193	$\alpha = -0\cdot80$
	o	964	952	947	938	917	892	846	738	524	214	$\beta = 1\cdot21$
	f_w	959	950	945	935	917	894	849	749	551	255	
Taiwan: males, 1959–60	f	964	935	927	910	879	842	785	680	471	157	$\alpha = -0\cdot62$
	o	955	925	919	908	889	857	801	674	442	162	$\beta = 1\cdot1$
	f_w	937	917	910	895	869	836	780	671	474	205	

TABLE 14B

Life table		1	5	10	20	30	40	50	60	70	80	α β
Mauritius: males, 1942–46	f	873	742	709	641	530	421	300	167	56	7	$\alpha = 0\cdot4$
	o	804	716	693	644	545	434	299	159	52	8	$\beta = 1\cdot6$
	f_w	773	671	648	609	546	472	383	274	147	40	
Guyana: males, 1945–47	f	938	880	864	831	771	700	602	446	227	46	$\alpha = -0\cdot1$
	o	902	864	852	831	783	718	601	424	210	60	$\beta = 1\cdot3$
	f_w	888	843	830	806	764	713	638	520	339	129	
Philippines: males, 1946–49	f	828	766	752	725	683	639	584	500	368	180	$\alpha = -0\cdot1$
	o	874	765	748	728	687	635	570	478	362	207	$\beta = 0\cdot7$
	f_s	860	780	763	741	703	660	600	502	338	121	
U.S.S.R.: females, 1926–27	f	786	723	710	684	644	604	554	481	365	196	$\alpha = -0\cdot0$
	o	828	729	705	683	646	605	558	489	366	186	$\beta = 0\cdot0$
	f_e	820	748	728	700	657	606	548	458	298	101	
Ceylon: males, 1952	f	898	855	845	826	793	758	711	635	498	267	$\alpha = -0\cdot4$
	o	911	853	833	822	801	772	726	643	487	244	$\beta = 0\cdot7$
	f_s	899	856	847	833	809	777	727	634	463	195	

The comparisons in Table 14A support the conclusions, drawn previously from the fitting of the logit system to average life tables. Again the adequacy of the method for describing the broad course of mortality but the limitations at one year and very late ages may be noted. For two of the life tables (Norway, Taiwan) the appropriate Regional set gives a poorer representation than the logit system and for another two (Japan and Czechoslovakia) the success is not much different. The observed mortality schedules of Table 14 B are better described by the logit system than the Regional sets, in all examples except Ceylon. The main reason is that the relationship between adult and child mortality is more extreme than for any of the Regional patterns. In the Mauritius and Guyana life tables adult death rates are very high compared with child rates and the reverse holds for the Philippines, U.S.S.R. and Ceylon. The Regional averages do not allow for such deviations in the "slope" of mortality and the measures from the fitted life tables of this system tend, therefore, to diverge from the observed values in the tails of the distribution outside the middle adult years. The β parameter in the logit system varies the slope and, as can be seen, permits the broad course of mortality with age to be represented even in these extreme life tables. Discrepancies at one year of age are, however, substantial and there are distortions of the observed curve from the theoretical linear relation on the logit scale. In view of the possible deficiencies in the reported death rates it is difficult to know what weight should be given to these deviations at particular ages.

The results in Tables 6 to 14 show that the logit system with the general standard can be used to represent the major features of recorded mortality patterns over the greater part of the age range. The accuracy of the system is less for infancy and at late years of life. It would be possible by adjustments to improve agreement at these ages but this has not been done here. There is much variability among populations with approximately the same level of mortality in the death rates reported at very early and late years. Some of the erratic features may be due to errors in the data but it is also the case that these are the ages of greatest vulnerability. It may be conjectured, therefore, that social and environmental factors in particular populations could lead to larger deviations from the model experience. Slight increases in the average accuracy of the logit system would be of little benefit for describing individual life tables and, for many purposes, would not justify the additional complication. Every life table calculated from observations has greater or lesser individual peculiarities. Clearly, no simple system of relations can hope to delineate these. When the same deviations occur consistently in groups of life tables, however, applications of the logit system can be strengthened by the use of special standards. An obvious example is in the study of changes in a population over time when a standard more closely related to the mortality characteristics of the particular community is preferable (see later). Again there is evidence, cumulatively convincing although each piece is weak, that in tropical African and some other developing countries death rates at under one year of age are relatively low compared with those in later childhood, notably at one to four years. An African standard life table for use as the base of the logit system has, therefore, been constructed and applied extensively in demographic studies of such countries.

Changes in Mortality Patterns with Level

The logistic function transforms a proportion lying between zero and one into a variable with a range of minus infinity to plus infinity. The "natural" way of trying to represent the relation between two sets of corresponding values on infinite scales is by polynomical functions beginning with a straight line. It is, perhaps, not too surprising that the linear relation between the logits of survivorship ratios is a reasonable description although there seems no logical basis for expecting it. The more surprising feature is that the steepness of the "slope" β varies about the central value of one over the whole range of recorded mortality levels. This is clear from the logit differences of the United Nations mortality schedules shown in Table 6 and also illustrated in Fig. 1. The slopes of the low and high mortality schedules (A and D) differ little; in view of the restricted choice of high mortality life tables of acceptable accuracy little weight can be laid on the apparent small difference. At intermediate levels of mortality (B and C) the slopes of the logit differences are negative, i.e. β is less than one. A possible explanation of this is suggested later. At any mortality level there are life tables for which β's depart from the central value, as is illustrated in Table 14, but the deviations have no very consistent association with the incidence of deaths.

Some of the features of the logit system, including the relation of

SWEDEN : MALES

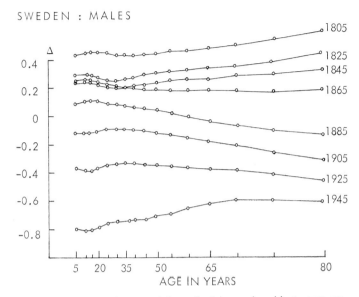

FIG. 2A. Differences from special standard in survivorship to ages on logit scale by time period.

SWEDEN : FEMALES

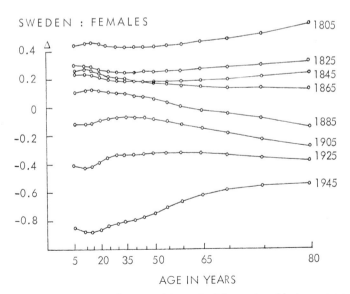

FIG. 2B. Differences from special standard in survivorship to ages on logit scale by time period.

slope to mortality level, are best seen by an examination of the movements of death rates over time in a single population. For the systematic trends to be separated from erratic fluctuations a long history of accurate records is needed. The data for Sweden are among the most suitable. Abridged life tables for Sweden were derived by normal techniques from the age specific death rates for decades beginning in 1801–10 and the logits of $(1 - l(x))$ obtained; no smoothing of measures was attempted. Special standard logits at ages were constructed by averaging over the range of life tables (male and female separately); the logit differences $D(x)$ between the life tables and the corresponding standard were calculated. The results are shown in Tables 15 and 16 for alternate decades only since this is sufficient to show the structure without the confusion of too many measures. The graphs of $D(x)$ against the appropriate logit standards are drawn in Figs. 2A and 2B, with the lines designated by the mid-point of the decade.

Despite the deviations for particular decades the representation of the life tables by straight lines on the logit scale gives a reasonable broad description. Apart from the early years the departures from linearity show little signs of systematic features which might suggest that a better model could be constructed simply. The addition of further parameters (e.g. by the use of higher order polynomials) would give a closer fit but it is clear that the overall improvement for each extra parameter would be very small. No insight into the nature of the relationship would thus be provided. The systematic deviations in the early years are of the kind, already discussed, which can be reduced by allowing for endogenous mortality in the first few weeks of life. A striking characteristic of the graphs is the similarity of the slopes for the earliest and latest decades although the trends are greatly different in some of the periods between. Thus the β values of the logit representation (on the special Swedish scales) are greater than one at high and low mortality levels but substantially less than one in some intermediate decades. It may be noted that the adoption of the general $Y_s(x)$ standard would not have modified these conclusions effectively but the resulting β's would have been rather lower, particularly for females. The broad movements in pattern with mortality level in the Swedish population, therefore, are consistent with the picture obtained from the structure of the United Nations average life-table schedules for different incidences of death.

Sweden, males

Age (x) (years)	l(x)								Logit average	Logit difference, D(x)							
	1801	1821	1841	1861	1881	1901	1921	1941		1801	1821	1841	1861	1881	1901	1921	1941
5	0·6795	0·7367	0·7570	0·7530	0·8053	0·8646	0·9133	0·9614	-0·8047	0·4289	0·2903	0·2365	0·2474	0·0948	-0·1223	-0·3726	-0·8029
10	0·6378	0·7083	0·7264	0·7184	0·7744	0·8473	0·9040	0·9565	-0·7276	0·4450	0·2843	0·2397	0·2596	0·1112	-0·1289	-0·3933	-0·8174
15	0·6142	0·6922	0·7102	0·7025	0·7594	0·8350	0·8961	0·9527	-0·6850	0·4525	0·2798	0·2368	0·2554	0·1103	-0·1257	-0·3923	-0·8164
20	0·5910	0·6750	0·6934	0·6855	0·7425	0·8162	0·8813	0·9452	-0·6310	0·4469	0·2656	0·2230	0·2414	0·1015	-0·1144	-0·3714	-0·7928
25	0·5596	0·6483	0·6693	0·6621	0·7184	0·7900	0·8608	0·9331	-0·5592	0·4394	0·2534	0·2067	0·2229	0·0909	-0·1033	-0·3518	-0·7585
30	0·5288	0·6177	0·6425	0·6380	0·6945	0·7657	0·8416	0·9227	-0·4939	0·4362	0·2540	0·2008	0·2106	0·0833	-0·0982	-0·3412	-0·7452
35	0·4972	0·5825	0·6115	0·6124	0·6712	0·7430	0·8229	0·9121	-0·4302	0·4358	0·2637	0·2034	0·2015	0·0734	-0·1006	-0·3379	-0·7396
40	0·4632	0·5431	0·5739	0·5830	0·6458	0·7186	0·8032	0·8997	-0·3623	0·4360	0·2759	0·2134	0·1947	0·0619	-0·1065	-0·3409	-0·7347
45	0·4248	0·4968	0·5306	0·5485	0·6158	0·6901	0·7802	0·8840	-0·2857	0·4372	0·2921	0·2244	0·1884	0·0498	-0·1146	-0·3477	-0·7297
50	0·3810	0·4452	0·4819	0·5077	0·5810	0·6567	0·7513	0·8609	-0·1973	0·4400	0·3073	0·2335	0·1819	0·0339	-0·1270	-0·3555	-0·7141
55	0·3283	0·3876	0·4249	0·4584	0·5397	0·6157	0·7143	0·8266	-0·0916	0·4495	0·3203	0·2429	0·1750	0·0120	-0·1441	-0·3666	-0·6893
60	0·2712	0·3259	0·3619	0·3993	0·4886	0·5652	0·6639	0·7765	0·0342	0·4601	0·3292	0·2493	0·1700	-0·0114	-0·1653	-0·3746	-0·6569
65	0·2077	0·2557	0·2924	0·3277	0·4246	0·5001	0·5945	0·7044	0·1914	0·4780	0·3428	0·2504	0·1679	-0·0395	-0·1916	-0·3827	-0·6256
70	0·1453	0·1833	0·2088	0·2464	0·3448	0·4165	0·5020	0·6028	0·3919	0·4941	0·3552	0·2742	0·1670	-0·0709	-0·2233	-0·3959	-0·6005
75	0·0832	0·1113	0·1293	0·1590	0·2479	0·3121	0·3830	0·4682	0·6597	0·5401	0·3791	0·2939	0·1731	-0·1047	-0·2645	-0·4213	-0·5960
80	0·0364	0·0521	0·0623	0·0802	0·1444	0·1937	0·2448	0·3040	1·0305	0·6076	0·4201	0·3253	0·1893	-0·1409	-0·3174	-0·4673	-0·6163

TABLE 16. Proportions surviving from birth in life tables for decades beginning in the year shown and corresponding logit differences; Sweden, females

Age (x) (years)	l(x)								Logit average	Logit difference, D(x)							
	1801	1821	1841	1861	1881	1901	1921	1941		1801	1821	1841	1861	1881	1901	1921	1941
5	0·7086	0·7640	0·7852	0·7768	0·8257	0·8830	0·9304	0·9699	-0·8906	0·4463	0·3032	0·2425	0·2671	0·1128	-0·1200	-0·4058	-0·8457
10	0·6684	0·7365	0·7567	0·7432	0·7946	0·8651	0·9215	0·9666	-0·8103	0·4598	0·2964	0·2429	0·2790	0·1338	-0·1188	-0·4211	-0·8723
15	0·6467	0·7204	0·7407	0·7276	0·7782	0·8507	0·9128	0·9637	-0·7628	0·4605	0·2896	0·2380	0·2716	0·1352	-0·1072	-0·4113	-0·8767
20	0·6235	0·7028	0·7232	0·7115	0·7607	0·8307	0·8980	0·9500	-0·7048	0·4526	0·2745	0·2246	0·2535	0·1265	-0·0905	-0·3828	-0·8588
25	0·5983	0·6807	0·7029	0·6925	0·7408	0·8080	0·8796	0·9417	-0·6405	0·4413	0·2620	0·2099	0·2346	0·1154	-0·0780	-0·3538	-0·8317
30	0·5704	0·6555	0·6807	0·6715	0·7187	0·7841	0·8612	0·9326	-0·5771	0·4354	0·2555	0·1986	0·2196	0·1081	-0·0678	-0·3355	-0·8140
35	0·5395	0·6267	0·6542	0·6479	0·6952	0·7602	0·8425	0·9219	-0·5129	0·4337	0·2539	0·1942	0·2080	0·1006	-0·0640	-0·3256	-0·8008
40	0·5054	0·5935	0·6233	0·6209	0·6696	0·7351	0·8229	0·9079	-0·4456	0·4348	0·2564	0·1938	0·1989	0·0924	-0·0648	-0·3225	-0·7886
45	0·4676	0·5567	0·5886	0·5905	0·6427	0·7088	0·8005	0·8879	-0·3735	0·4484	0·2596	0·1944	0·1905	0·0800	-0·0713	-0·3212	-0·7706
50	0·4293	0·5182	0·5523	0·5577	0·6142	0·6801	0·7734	0·8591	-0·2966	0·4490	0·2602	0·1916	0·1807	0·0641	-0·0805	-0·3172	-0·7381
55	0·3811	0·4713	0·5066	0·5178	0·5805	0·6465	0·7386	0·8178	-0·2045	0·4470	0·2620	0·1913	0·1689	0·0421	-0·0973	-0·3149	-0·6994
60	0·3261	0·4159	0·4505	0·4664	0·5374	0·6040	0·6940	0·7559	-0·0933	0·4563	0·2631	0·1926	0·1606	0·0184	-0·1178	-0·3161	-0·6575
65	0·2581	0·3426	0·3805	0·3989	0·4789	0·5474	0·6322	0·6628	0·0517	0·4752	0·2742	0·1920	0·1533	-0·0095	-0·1468	-0·3225	-0·6168
70	0·1881	0·2594	0·2892	0·3145	0·4001	0·4696	0·5443	0·5443	0·2414	0·4838	0·2832	0·2082	0·1481	-0·0439	-0·1805	-0·3302	-0·5793
75	0·1143	0·1692	0·1899	0·2178	0·3000	0·3647	0·4262	0·4262	0·4976	0·5252	0·2981	0·2277	0·1417	-0·0740	-0·2201	-0·3489	-0·5506
80	0·0520	0·0866	0·0989	0·1211	0·1880	0·2375	0·2799	0·3539	0·8517	0·5969	0·3262	0·2531	0·1393	-0·1202	-0·2685	-0·3793	-0·5507

Table 17. Proportions surviving from birth in life tables for quinquennia beginning in the year shown and corresponding logit differences; England and Wales, males

Age (x) (years)	$l(x)$									
	1866	1876	1886	1896	1906	1916	1926	1936	1946	1956
5	0·7194	0·7376	0·7557	0·7560	0·8042	0·8357	0·8866	0·9176	0·9449	0·9693
10	0·6916	0·7146	0·7376	0·7407	0·7909	0·8200	0·8757	0·9089	0·9407	0·9669
15	0·6769	0·7024	0·7274	0·7321	0·7831	0·8101	0·8687	0·9034	0·9375	0·9650
20	0·6569	0·6856	0·7126	0·7191	0·7716	0·7931	0·8575	0·8943	0·9319	0·9608
25	0·6301	0·6630	0·6933	0·7017	0·7564	0·7714	0·8435	0·8820	0·9245	0·9554
30	0·6006	0·6360	0·6702	0·6815	0·7381	0·7464	0·8287	0·8698	0·9162	0·9504
35	0·5690	0·6048	0·6420	0·6571	0·7160	0·7204	0·8129	0·8567	0·9069	0·9444
40	0·5339	0·5689	0·6077	0·6266	0·6887	0·6928	0·7919	0·8396	0·8953	0·9355
45	0·4955	0·5276	0·5671	0·5885	0·6544	0·6619	0·7641	0·8162	0·8780	0·9213
50	0·4531	0·4820	0·5191	0·5431	0·6105	0·6236	0·7273	0·7824	0·8491	0·8974
55	0·4050	0·4294	0·4638	0·4874	0·5558	0·5742	0·6796	0·7318	0·8047	0·8554
60	0·3497	0·3691	0·3976	0·4211	0·4859	0·5115	0·6157	0·6622	0·7373	0·7845
65	0·2860	0·2993	0·3227	0·3429	0·4024	0·4299	0·5283	0·5679	0·6405	0·6819
70	0·2147	0·2233	0·2381	0·2571	0·3056	0·3308	0·4156	0·4511	0·5189	0·5476
75	0·1414	0·1458	0·1550	0·1685	0·2036	0·2193	0·2846	0·3111	0·3742	0·3892
80	0·0760	0·0777	0·0827	0·0917	0·1128	0·1154	0·1534	0·1677	0·2228	0·2299

TABLE 17 (*continued*)

Age (x) (years)	Logit average	Logit difference, D(x)									
		1866	1876	1886	1896	1906	1916	1926	1936	1946	1956
5	−0·9018	0·4310	0·3849	0·3372	0·3264	0·1956	0·0884	−0·1266	−0·3035	−0·5191	−0·8244
10	−0·8524	0·4486	0·3935	0·3357	0·3276	0·1872	0·0944	−0·1237	−0·2978	−0·5299	−0·8356
15	−0·8235	0·4537	0·3941	0·3327	0·3207	0·1815	0·0980	−0·1211	−0·2944	−0·5304	−0·8350
20	−0·7792	0·4544	0·3894	0·3251	0·3091	0·1706	0·1073	−0·1182	−0·2884	−0·5288	−0·8201
25	−0·7248	0·4584	0·3865	0·3169	0·2971	0·1583	0·1166	−0·1174	−0·2811	−0·5276	−0·8076
30	−0·6685	0·4645	0·3895	0·3141	0·2881	0·1504	0·1288	−0·1198	−0·2811	−0·5272	−0·8074
35	−0·6087	0·4698	0·3959	0·3167	0·2835	0·1463	0·1356	−0·1259	−0·2855	−0·5297	−0·8071
40	−0·5393	0·4714	0·4007	0·3205	0·2805	0·1422	0·1328	−0·1289	−0·2881	−0·5335	−0·7975
45	−0·4565	0·4655	0·4012	0·3215	0·2776	0·1374	0·1206	−0·1311	−0·2889	−0·5305	−0·7735
50	−0·3550	0·4491	0·3909	0·3168	0·2687	0·1302	0·1026	−0·1356	−0·2849	−0·5086	−0·7291
55	−0·2304	0·4226	0·3725	0·3029	0·2557	0·1183	0·0809	−0·1455	−0·2715	−0·4774	−0·6586
60	−0·0784	0·3885	0·3465	0·2862	0·2375	0·1065	0·0554	−0·1572	−0·2581	−0·4377	−0·5675
65	0·1054	0·3520	0·3198	0·2653	0·2198	0·0923	0·0357	−0·1621	−0·2421	−0·3941	−0·4866
70	0·3281	0·3204	0·2950	0·2533	0·2026	0·0823	0·0241	−0·1576	−0·2301	−0·3659	−0·4237
75	0·6090	0·2929	0·2751	0·2391	0·1893	0·0730	0·0258	−0·1481	−0·2116	−0·3520	−0·3837
80	0·9769	0·2723	0·2598	0·2262	0·1695	0·0541	0·0414	−0·1227	−0·1759	−0·3521	−0·3723

TABLE 18. Proportions surviving from birth in life tables for quinquennia beginning in the year shown and corresponding logit differences; England and Wales, females

Age (x) (year)	$l(x)$ 1866	1876	1886	1896	1906	1916	1926	1936	1946	1956
5	0·7480	0·7685	0·7855	0·7869	0·8312	0·8603	0·9074	0·9344	0·9566	0·9761
10	0·7209	0·7463	0·7667	0·7707	0·8171	0·8441	0·8972	0·9267	0·9535	0·9745
15	0·7056	0·7333	0·7555	0·7615	0·8086	0·8333	0·8904	0·9218	0·9509	0·9732
20	0·6833	0·7151	0·7400	0·7488	0·7975	0·8182	0·8797	0·9136	0·9460	0·9714
25	0·6572	0·6931	0·7211	0·7334	0·7842	0·8001	0·8669	0·9027	0·9388	0·9688
30	0·6283	0·6667	0·6981	0·7148	0·7685	0·7787	0·8531	0·8915	0·9309	0·9656
35	0·5971	0·6371	0·6711	0·6922	0·7492	0·7574	0·8384	0·8797	0·9224	0·9610
40	0·5639	0·6040	0·6397	0·6648	0·7258	0·7352	0·8211	0·8654	0·9123	0·9542
45	0·5287	0·5676	0·6039	0·6316	0·6965	0·7103	0·7999	0·8472	0·8990	0·9435
50	0·4910	0·5280	0·5630	0·5927	0·6597	0·6795	0·7723	0·8221	0·8791	0·9270
55	0·4481	0·4821	0·5152	0·5448	0·6141	0·6389	0·7344	0·7867	0·8504	0·9022
60	0·3968	0·4262	0·4548	0·4855	0·5541	0·5872	0·6835	0·7380	0·8090	0·8651
65	0·3345	0·3582	0·3825	0·4105	0·4786	0·5180	0·6102	0·6657	0·7467	0·8072
70	0·2607	0·2788	0·2954	0·3223	0·3831	0·4272	0·5116	0·5647	0·6553	0·7188
75	0·1803	0·1917	0·2037	0·2239	0·2736	0·3135	0·3824	0·4298	0·5214	0·5874
80	0·1028	0·1101	0·1167	0·1317	0·1657	0·1880	0·2368	0·2714	0·3530	0·4136

Table 18 (*continued*)

Age (x) (years)	Logit average	Logit difference, $D(x)$									
		1866	1876	1886	1896	1906	1916	1926	1936	1946	1956
5	−1·0024	0·4585	0·4023	0·3534	0·3492	0·2051	0·0935	−0·1388	−0·3258	−0·5437	−0·8533
10	−0·9492	0·4748	0·4098	0·3544	0·3430	0·2009	0·1049	−0·1343	−0·3193	−0·5612	−0·8731
15	−0·9171	0·4800	0·4114	0·3530	0·3366	0·1968	0·1124	−0·1303	−0·3161	−0·5648	−0·8787
20	−0·8718	0·4872	0·4117	0·3489	0·3257	0·1866	0·1197	−0·1231	−0·3075	−0·5594	−0·8901
25	−0·8187	0·4933	0·4113	0·3438	0·3127	0·1734	0·1253	−0·1181	−0·2953	−0·5463	−0·9001
30	−0·7617	0·4993	0·4151	0·3425	0·3024	0·1618	0·1327	−0·1178	−0·2914	−0·5383	−0·9061
35	−0·7014	0·5047	0·4200	0·3447	0·2962	0·1542	0·1321	−0·1218	−0·2930	−0·5360	−0·9014
40	−0·6348	0·5062	0·4237	0·3477	0·2924	0·1481	0·1242	−0·1271	−0·2954	−0·5363	−0·8835
45	−0·5588	0·5013	0·4229	0·3479	0·2893	0·1435	0·1103	−0·1340	−0·2978	−0·5345	−0·8490
50	−0·4696	0·4877	0·4134	0·3429	0·2821	0·1386	0·0940	−0·1411	−0·2958	−0·5225	−0·7989
55	−0·3639	0·4681	0·3998	0·3335	0·2741	0·1315	0·0786	−0·1447	−0·2886	−0·5048	−0·7473
60	−0·2361	0·4456	0·3848	0·3267	0·2651	0·1275	0·0598	−0·1489	−0·2817	−0·4856	−0·6930
65	−0·0762	0·4203	0·3678	0·3156	0·2572	0·1189	0·0401	−0·1478	−0·2681	−0·4644	−0·6397
70	0·1244	0·3969	0·3509	0·3104	0·2471	0·1137	0·0223	−0·1475	−0·2546	−0·4456	−0·5938
75	0·3821	0·3751	0·3373	0·2994	0·2396	0·1061	0·0097	−0·1426	−0·2407	−0·4250	−0·5587
80	0·7179	0·3654	0·3268	0·2943	0·2251	0·0904	0·0135	−0·1327	−0·2241	−0·4149	−0·5434

Similar measures for England and Wales are given in Tables 17 and 18 and illustrated in Figs. 3A and 3B. The life tables used were those computed by Case *et al.* (1962) and are for five year time periods. Much the same general conclusions are reached from these measures as for the Swedish observations but the higher values of β for the earlier life tables, comparable to the slope in recent years, do not appear. The England and Wales life tables, however, are shown from 1856–60, as against the Swedish 1801–10, and begin at a lower mortality level. The steep slope of the measures for England and Wales males in the most recent period is also notable, reflecting the relatively high death rates at later adult ages compared with the mortality in childhood.

Interpretation of Logit Relations

Our aim has been to demonstrate that the relations between mortality patterns in different populations can be broadly described by a two parameter linear equation in the logits of survivorship proportions. The simplicity of the result prompts a search for further elucidation, in particular of the meaning of the α and β parameters. It was mentioned earlier that the logit function was used in standard techniques of bio-assay. A comparison of these applications with the system presented here is instructive. The bio-assay procedures (Finney, 1952) are for the measurement of drug potencies by the treatment of experimental animals. The response of the animal to a large enough dose of the drug is death or some other qualitative end result. The probability of animals dying at drug level z (usually measured as the logarithm of the dose) is taken to have a symmetrical one-peaked distribution. For different preparations of the drug or batches of animals the mean and spread of the distribution are assumed to be variable but the shape to remain the same. Several forms of distribution have been used in applications but two are much the most common. In one the shape of the probability distribution of deaths at dose z is described by the function $\frac{1}{2} \operatorname{sech}^2 (\alpha + \beta z)$. Here the mean of the drug levels at death is $-\alpha/\beta$ and the standard deviation (the measure of spread) is $1/\beta$. If we now consider the proportion of animals which require a dose of more than z to kill them and call this $l(z)$, the distribution gives:

$$\tfrac{1}{2} \log_e \frac{1 - l(z)}{l(z)} = \alpha + \beta z.$$

ENGLAND AND WALES: MALES

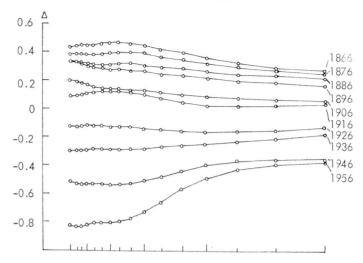

FIG. 3A. Differences from special standard in survivorship to ages on logit scale by time period.

ENGLAND AND WALES: FEMALES

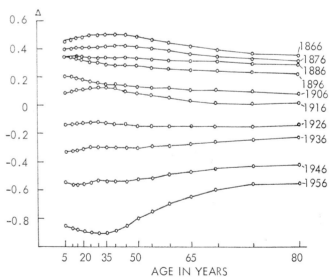

FIG. 3B. Differences from special standard in survivorship to ages on logit scale by time period.

H

The analogy with the logit system of life tables is clear. If we regard

$$Y_s(x) = \tfrac{1}{2} \log_e \frac{1 - l_s(x)}{l_s(x)}$$

as a transformation of the age scale x (just as in bio-assay the drug dose is normally transformed by the logarithm) the equation $Y(x) = \alpha + \beta Y_s(x)$ is formally the same as appears in bio-assay.

It is thus possible to interpret the logit system in the following way. On an appropriate scale the probability of death at a given age (or dose of life as it were) can be described by a symmetrical, one peaked distribution. For different populations the shape of this distribution is the same but its location and spread vary. The mean $-\alpha/\beta$ can be taken as a convenient measure of mortality level. Note that on transformation back to the original scale it specifies the age to which half the births survive. The system has been arranged so that the central value of the standard deviation $1/\beta$ is close to one. High values of β indicate a relatively low spread of ages at death and vice versa. There is no consistent tendency for the location of the distribution and its spread to be associated.

The other probability function widely used in bio-assay is the ubiquitous Normal or Gaussian distribution. Corresponding to the logit for describing proportions requiring a dose of more than z to kill them there is now the probit. Probits cannot be as simply expressed as logits although they are not necessarily, with appropriate tables, more difficult to apply. For most practical purposes the results obtained by using logits and probits in bio-assay studies are effectively identical. Differences only occur at the extreme tails of the distribution. An obvious question for consideration is whether human mortality patterns would be better described by a probit system than by logits. The indications are that they might be if an adjustment was introduced for endogenous deaths in the early weeks of life but the improvement would be slight and so far as can be seen of no practical consequence. Since the logit function is known to demographers from other uses in population studies there seems no reason to change over to a probit system.

It is convenient, however, for the exposition in the following paragraph to assume that the underlying distribution is Normal because the properties of this function are familiar to biologists. On the transformed scale, the length of life z of an individual in a population is then a Normally distributed random variable. z can now be expressed schematically as a sum of Normally distributed random variables where each component contributes its share to the spread of ages at death. For example we might represent the age at death as:

$$z = u + v + w$$

where u is a genetic component, v the effect of the environment in its widest sense, including socio-economic factors and medical services, and w an individual chance variability or "error". Further breakdowns can easily be imagined. The u genetic component would be relatively stable both in mean and standard deviation in a given population over time but might differ among populations. It would be expected that the major changes and differentials would be in v; w would have a zero mean but its standard deviation might vary considerably over populations. Interactions of u and v could also be incorporated. The lower values of β observed at intermediate levels of mortality implying a wider spread in z might plausibly be explained by changes in v. A speculative interpretation would be that as the "environment" began to improve the effects did not reach all groups in the population at the same time and greater heterogeneity, resulting in a lower β, followed. At a later stage as benefits became more evenly distributed, the value of β would tend to rise. There is, of course, plenty of direct evidence of mortality differentials among population sub-groups classified by social and economic characteristics. It is tempting to explain the extreme values of β for some life tables in terms of the degree of homogeneity (geographical, economic and social) of the particular countries. There seems to be some justification for this but mainly of an impressionistic nature. The probability distribution of v could also be much modified by changes in environmental factors which bore with unequal weight at different stages of life, e.g. malarial conditions or smoke pollution.

A Scale of Mortality Movements

It has been demonstrated that the "norm" for changes in mortality patterns is a simple shift in the location of the mean of a distribution when an appropriate transformation of the age variable has been made. In certain circumstances, systematic movements over time in the spread of the distribution may occur. Other deviations are of a local and more transient nature. The logit system thus provides a meaningful scale for assessing changes in mortality by age, e.g. for weighing the import of an 80 per cent fall in death rates at 15–19 years against a 10 per cent drop at 75–79 years. The kind of guidance provided can be illustrated by reference again to the logit difference curves for Sweden in Graphs 2A and 2B. The vertical distance between successive curves at any given age is a measure, on our scale, of the cumulated difference in mortality up to that point. Parallel curves imply movements in death rates over time which are consistent for all age groups. A widening distance can be interpreted as meaning that over the range where it happens the change in mortality is greater than the average effect for earlier ages. Thus in Sweden, between 1805 and 1945, the fall in mortality on our scale was much the same at all ages and for men as for women; young females up to about 20 years old did slightly better than other sections. The pattern of changes over the century and a half, however, varied greatly by age group. Between 1825 and 1865 falls in death rates were modest at all ages but the young did particularly badly. The big improvement at older years was from 1865 to 1885; at early ages the decrease in mortality in the 1905–45 period was considerably larger than in the whole of the preceding century. The curvature of the line draws attention to more localized features. For example, the changing shape of the kinks in adolescence and early adulthood reflects the relative reduction in tuberculosis but increase in accidents as causes of death. The tendency, in more recent periods for improvement in mortality at 50–70 years to lag behind the changes at other ages is apparent from the sharp narrowing of curve intervals in this range.

Projections of Future Mortality

The logit system provides a useful tool for the projection of future mortality from past trends because the two parameters are sufficiently few for efficient estimation from observations but flexible enough to describe a realistic range of possibilities (Brass, 1969). This application does not depend on the meaning of the parameters. If, however, we are prepared to accept the broad validity of the interpretation proposed, it follows that over long enough periods changes in mortality will consist mainly in a shift of the location of the "death curve" on the transformed age scale, i.e. in α while β will tend to return to near its central value. On this hypothesis, we can look at patterns of future mortality if death rates continue to fall below the lowest levels at present reached. In most, if not all, developed countries, the recent tendency has been for β to increase, particularly for males, because of the relatively small decrease in mortality at late middle ages. The assumption that the main movement, over a long period, will be in α implies that the resistance to improvement at these ages is a temporary feature. Table 19 shows selected measures for life tables of the logit system with $\beta = 1$ and α taken beyond the limits recorded for any populations. The example with $\alpha = -1.0$, has roughly the present mortality level in highly developed countries. For equal decreases in α, the increment in e_0 the expectation of life at birth (the usual measure of overall mortality) is reduced both relatively and absolutely with greater longevity. Thus a movement of α from -1.0 to -2.0 increases the expectation of life by 14 years from 70.7 to 84.7, or only half the rise from 43.4 to 70.7 years, which accompanies a shift of α from zero to -1.0. This gives a numerical scale to the greater difficulty of increasing life expectancy when death rates are already low compared to the larger scope in high mortality populations. Although the situation is complicated by changes in β, it does not seem that the pace of the shift in α is now accelerating in low mortality populations. We would anticipate, therefore, that future rises in life

TABLE 19. Survivors from 10,000 births in logit model life tables with different values of α ($\beta = 1.0$) (e_0 is expectation of life at birth)

Age (years)	α					
	0.5	0.0	-0.5	-1.0	-1.5	-2.0
0	10,000	10,000	10,000	10,000	10,000	10,000
1	6,756	8,499	9,390	9,767	9,913	9,968
5	5,506	7,691	9,005	9,610	9,853	9,945
15	5,066	7,362	8,835	9,538	9,825	9,935
25	4,417	6,826	8,539	9,408	9,774	9,916
35	3,774	6,223	8,175	9,241	9,707	9,890
45	3,132	5,535	7,712	9,016	9,614	9,854
55	2,375	4,585	6,971	8,622	9,445	9,788
65	1,482	3,210	5,624	7,774	9,047	9,627
75	610	1,500	3,242	5,660	7,800	9,060
85	109	290	751	1,808	3,750	6,199
95	4	10	27	73	197	518
e_0	26.86	43.44	58.94	70.73	78.94	84.65

expectancy will become increasingly slow, *even although on the logit scale mortality continues to fall as fast as before* and the proportional improvement in death rates at younger ages is large. In both Sweden and England and Wales α has changed by one unit in some 80 years and by half a unit in the last 35 years. The pattern in the example of Table 19 with α equal to −1·5 may indicate broadly the situation in Western Europe at the end of the century. Compared with the life table for α equal to −1·0, mortality up to age five has fallen from 39 out of a 1000 births to less than 15 and the proportion of persons who reach age 65 years has increased from 78 per cent to 90 per cent. However, the expectation of life at age 85 has only risen from 3·8 years to 4·2.

References

BENJAMIN, B. (1964) Demographic aspects of ageing, with special reference to England and Wales, *J. Inst. Actuaries* **90**(3), 211–253.

BRASS, W., *et al.* (1968) *The Demography of Tropical Africa*, Princeton University Press, New Jersey.

BRASS, W. (1969) A generation method for projecting death rates, *Population Growth and the Brain Drain*, edited by F. Bechofer, University Press, Edinburgh, pp. 75–91.

CASE, R. A. M., *et al.* (1962) *Serial Abridged Life Tables: England and Wales 1841–1960*, Chester Beatty Research Institute, London.

COALE, A. J. and DEMENY, P. (1966) *Regional Model Life Tables and Stable Populations*, Princeton University Press, New Jersey.

FINNEY, D. J. (1952) *Statistical Method in Bioassay*, Charles Griffin & Co., London.

FISHER, R. A. and YATES, F. (1963) *Statistical Tables for Biological, Agricultural and Medical Research*, 6th edition, Oliver & Boyd, Edinburgh.

KERMACK, W. O., MCKENDRICK, A. G. and MCKINLAY, P. L. (1934) Death Rates in Great Britain and Sweden, *Lancet* **1**, 698–703.

LEDERMANN, S. and BREAS, J. (1959) Les dimensions de la mortalité, *Population*, Paris, 14th year, (4), 637–682.

PEARSON, K. (1948) *Karl Pearson's Early Statistical Papers*, Cambridge University Press.

UNITED NATIONS (1955) *Age and Sex Patterns of Mortality: Model Life Tables for Underdeveloped Countries*, New York.

UNITED NATIONS (1962) Factor analysis and sex–age–specific death rates: a contribution to the study of the dimensions of mortality, *Popul. Bull. U.N.* No. 6, 147–201.

UNITED NATIONS (1948–67) *Demographic Year Books*, New York.

PALAEODEMOGRAPHY

DON R. BROTHWELL

British Museum (Natural History)

PALAEODEMOGRAPHY may be defined briefly as the study of the demography of past populations, and especially of prehistoric and protohistoric communities. For the most part it relies upon the direct study of human remains, although archaeological data* and semi-documentary evidence—that is, ethnohistory† may at times also be pertinent.

It is thus not out of place to have this subject included in a general symposium on demography, even though the methods and problems of studying the vital statistics of recent groups are rather different from those used in the analysis of the ancient dead. Indeed, with the fast disappearance of primitive communities today, it may soon become one of the few ways of getting demographic information about such peoples.

To expand on these differences a little; the demographer of recent man can hope to have information on the nature and size of a group, and can hope to be able to sample at one or various points in time; to have full data on the sexes, and except for primitive aboriginal groups, to have fairly accurate ages for his people. In contrast, palaeodemography is usually uncertain of group size at any moment in time, and is most unlikely to have detailed information on social stratification, family size, population composition and so on. The

---

* For example, Schwartz (1956) undertook population estimates for Cohonina peoples in Arizona (600–1200) from the evidence of pottery. Similarly, Turner and Lofgren (1966) attempt to estimate household size and population trends between 500–1900, again on the evidence of pottery. A different type of population information is seen in Willey's (1956) study of house occupation through time at a site in Honduras.

† A good example in this field is the recent Huxley Memorial Lecture by J. Eric Thompson (1967).

accuracy of age estimation depends upon the nature of the material, and is more open to error in the adult age groups than in children. The reverse of this is the case in sex determination, where skeletal remains of children still defy accurate sexing, and in adults precision is proportionate to the amount of skeletal material available for study. However, my task here is not to elaborate on these difficulties, but to show the sort of information which has so far been obtained. Perhaps the best order of reviewing the biological aspects of palaeodemography is to begin with a general consideration of the world population through time, followed by details of life expectancy, age composition, and divisions by sex.

Finally, it would seem important to consider, albeit briefly, the possible relevance of studies on ancient disease to the demography of these earlier groups.

Total and Regional Population Estimates

Various attempts have been made to estimate world and regional population numbers, even back into Palaeolithic times. Although, of course these projections back into time can only be very tentative, I think they have some value in, for example, suggesting the thinness of population spread at a particular period, or in the case of the New World to emphasize the extent of the pre-contact population growth and post-contact decimation.

Views on these past trends have crystallized somewhat during the past three decades. Pearl and Gould (1936) considered three hypotheses for the history of world population growth and failed in all of them to realize that prior to the population explosion with the coming of the industrial revolution, there was an earlier and no less significant one associated with the development of agriculture some 8000 years ago. For the first time, family units could concentrate far beyond the limits dictated previously by a hunting and collecting economy*, and as the development of higher cultures in both the Old and New Worlds shows, this resulted in considerable population increase and concentration in some areas. In terms of numbers this probably meant a leap of over 50,000,000 in the three or four millennia following the Mesolithic Period. By the expansion of the Roman Empire, the total had increased perhaps to 150,000,000, with

* Coon (1959) argues for Pleistocene hunting communities being no more than 80 to 100 breeding family units.

a differential fertility probably strongly weighted towards groups exploiting the better soils and with social organizations capable of making full use of the revolution in plant and animal domestication. Certainly, regions such as Eastern Asia, the Mediterranean World, and Meso-America must have been expanding far more rapidly than most other areas (Fig. 1).

Age at Death and Age-Group Variations

Demographic interest in the age at death of earlier peoples has a relatively long history. Pearson (1902) compared the ages of a small series of Egyptian mummies with recent English data. Macdonell (1913) analysed over 10,000 ages gathered from Roman inscriptions. From these, representing four regions of the Mediterranean area, he was able to demonstrate life expectancy differences between the early groups and recent data, and he also noted a marked contrast between the Ancient Roman and North African samples. Only 11 per cent of the Romans in Italy survived to 60 years, whereas in North Africa a figure of over 40 per cent reached this age—at least so the inscriptions suggest.

In considering the results derived from skeletal studies, some of the factors limiting the extent and accuracy of this type of work should perhaps first be mentioned. First of all, the criteria used in ageing skeletons are still being modified and added to. Recent work includes the estimation of fairly precise ages in young infants by reference to the daily incremental cross-striations of the enamel prisms in developing teeth (Boyde, 1963); while Kerley (1965) has demonstrated that there are also measurable microscopic age changes in the cortex of the major long bones which can be used in age estimations.

Prior to Upper Pleistocene times all age estimates, whether on children or adults are open to considerable doubt. Schultz (1960) has pointed out that the further we go towards a pre-hominid form, the more developmental times must be reduced—until in fact they become more comparable with the range known in the great apes today. Thus, to consider the immature Taung specimen as being a "six year old" or the Olduvai child as "eleven years" may well be science fiction, and there is surely much cause to doubt the developmental age estimates for the 500,000 year old *Homo erectus* children also. But to return to post-Pleistocene times, considerable care is still

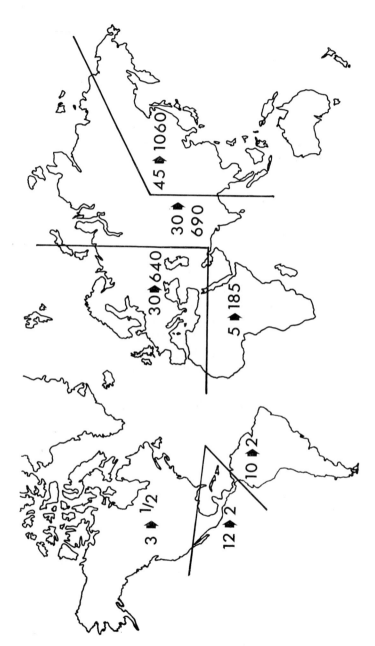

FIG. 1. Regional population changes during the past two thousand years. The figure before the arrow is for c. 30 B.C., and the right-hand one is for the present. Numbers represent estimates in millions The New World figures fail to indicate the total expansion to perhaps 100,000,000 just prior to European contact.

needed in assessing the reliability of the age data—if rather for other reasons. Burial environment can selectively eliminate infant remains, so that soil conditions must be considered. In some cultures, recent (for instance among Bushmen) and ancient (as in Romano-British times), still-born and newborn infants may be buried away from the usual cemetery area. All too often in palaeodemographic work this is not sufficiently considered, with the result that the vital statistics derived from the available age data may be open to question. One rough method of testing whether the skeletal assemblage has too few young infants to represent a "normal" population, is to consider the proportion of under one year olds relative to the total under 20 years (Fig. 2)*.

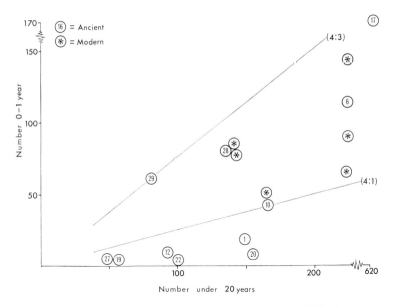

FIG. 2. Frequency of those under 1 year against those under 20 in eleven ancient populations. A few modern series have been scaled down to similar sample sizes to show that the ratio of these two age groups seems normally to be between 4 : 3 and 4 : 1. Encircled numbers refer to sites listed in the appendix.

* This would seem a more sensitive method than merely considering the child/ adult ratio, although often the published age data permit this but do not give children under one year.

Eleven early groups were plotted in this way, and for comparison six recent samples were "scaled down" to fit the diagram. It will be seen that only five early series are likely to have an unbiassed proportion of infants under one year. The others are suspect, and it is possible that groups 27, 12, and 20 (all from England and Ireland) are heavily influenced by detrimental soil conditions. Group 19 is a pooled series from British Neolithic barrows, and here there may

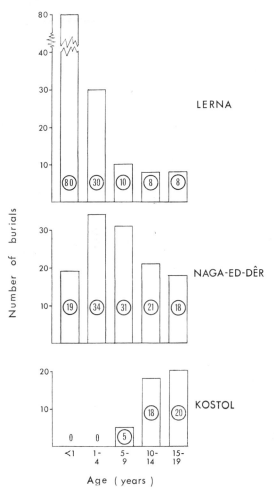

Fig. 3. Frequency of non-adults in various age groups, from Lerna in Greece, Naga-ed-dêr in Egypt, and Kostol in Nubia.

well have been social factors operating against child burial in these special tombs. Groups 22 and 1 are from Egypt and Nubia, and the bias may again reflect burial practices more than anything else. Group 1, a Predynastic series from Naga-ed-Dêr is also seen in Fig. 3, where five age divisions are given for those under 20 years. It is clear in this figure that the Naga-ed-Dêr under-one-year column may be as much as half of its true height, whereas the other columns look biologically acceptable. In comparison, the Bronze Age series from Lerna, in Greece, shows particularly high infant mortality in the first column, and seems most unlikely to be misrepresenting the situation in this Greek population. In contrast to both of these is the child data from Kostol in Nubia (X-group burials; c. 350–500). In this case we know fairly certainly that the tombs contained both upper and lower classes of individual (Batrawi, 1935), but the majority were people sacrificed at the burial of one or other chieftain (young children being excluded from this religious privilege). There can of course be the reverse of this and Bullen (1963) suggests that multiple infant burials from the Goodman Mound, Florida (c. 1500–1600), have ritual significance, and supports this claim by details of the differential fracturing of the skull in these skeletons and by ethnohistorical accounts.

So far, few sites have yielded a sufficiently large and well stratified series of skeletons to permit separation into two or more periods. This is not entirely the fault of the type of cemetery, for there is still far from an optimal working relationship between archaeologist and human biologist—but there are exceptions. The two prehistoric cultural components of the Amerindian burial area on Hiwassee Island (Lewis and Kneberg, 1940) show age-group differences (Table) which may be indicative of a demographic change (although only 273 burials are represented).

TABLE. Age composition in per cent of the prehistoric Hiwassee Island Burials

	Under 20 yrs.	20–30	30–40	40+ yrs.
Hamilton component	40·0	30·0	13·6	16·4
Dallas component	70·5	10·4	11·7	7·4

Possibly a better example is the recently excavated stratified Christian cemetery at Meinarti in Nubia. Here, two groups were separated, representing two successive 50 year periods (Fig. 4). The age-groups show frequency differences which are at present being analysed in relation to certain cultural factors (Armelagos, 1965).

Regrettably even less is known of long-term trends in differential mortality for any one particular region, and for some time Angel's (1947, 1954) work on early Greek societies was all that could be quoted. But interest is at last on the increase, and Kobayashi's (1967) work on early Japanese series shows what can be done even with rather unpromising looking material.

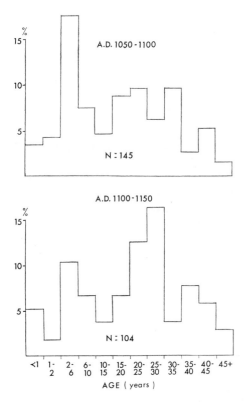

FIG. 4. Age composition in Mediaeval Nubian cemetery group, showing possible differences in mortality between two successive periods. Armelagos (1965).

Mean Life Span

In calculating a precise average length of life for an early population, one should not only have all those dying in each age-group, but also a well-established age for each person. Because this is not possible in palaeodemographic work, life expectancy estimates must be regarded as much cruder than their counterpart on modern peoples. Also, regrettably, procedural anarchy is still the rule in this field, so that we now have varied life expectancy figures for all ages combined (whether or not there are too few infants in the series!), for post-puberty individuals, and for adults*. However, some general conclusions can still be drawn from such data.

Taking first the longevity estimates on teenagers and adults† the averages for the various series prior to A.D. 1600 range from just under 30 years to a little over 40 years. Much of the variation within this 10 year period may reflect inadequacy of sample size or minor differences in the standards used in age determination. An exception is the work of Angel (1954), whose detailed studies on Greek series from 3500 B.C. to A.D. 1750 show a gradually increasing life expectancy from 31 to 40 years up to Classical times and then a 10 year decline in average longevity to the Turkish period (A.D. 1400). Thus, this data suggests that, prior to the industrial revolution, very few populations are likely to have an average length of life exceeding 40 years.

With regard to longevity estimates which include *all* children, most at present seem open to question, but with a few exceptions. The prehistoric Indian Knoll series from Kentucky has an average of 18·6 years (Johnston and Snow, 1961). The two well-excavated and extensive Mediaeval cemeteries of Aebelholt Abbey in Denmark and Westerhus in Sweden are interesting, in that the average life span at Westerhus was 17·7 years, very close to the Kentucky mean, but was as high as 32·2 years for the Danish series (Møller-Christensen, 1958; Gejvall, 1960). Fairly certainly this was the result of the Danish group being a combination of local villagers and "intrusive" adults belonging to the Augustinian order.

---

* Most of the comparative data are contained in Angel (1947), Dublin, *et al.* (1949), Goldstein (1953), Vallois (1960), Gejvall (1960), Howells (1960) and Kobayashi (1967).

† I am excluding here the longevity estimates calculated by Senyurek (1957) from the data on Roman inscriptions by Macdonell (1913). These may well represent only the higher social strata.

Sex Differences in some Vital Statistics

Although some physical anthropologists have attempted to differentiate the sexes even in young children, it is generally still regarded as very hazardous to attempt this division other than in adults (and certainly prior to adolescence). However, this still leaves plenty of scope for group analysis. As in the case of the child/adult ratio, it would seem important to establish initially whether the early populations show a sex bias beyond the range of variation seen in recent communities. In Fig. 5, twenty-seven early series are plotted to show the numbers of males and females present The result is encouraging in that the majority cluster along the line of sexual equality, there being a slight predominance of males in 18 groups.

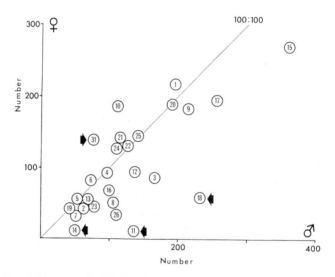

FIG. 5. Number of adult females plotted against the number of adult males, for twenty-seven early series. The four arrowed groups receive special mention in the text. Numbers within the circles refer to sites given in the appendix.

Some of the samples are clearly anomalous, and this raises the question again of the possible archaeologically biassed nature of the material received for analysis. Figure 6 shows the plan of a totally excavated Dark Age cemetery in Somerset, the symbols separating young from adult males and females. It seems reasonable to accept

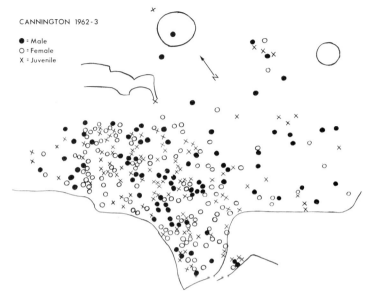

FIG. 6. General plan of a Dark Age cemetery at Cannington, Somerset, showing the random scatter of males, females and immature individuals.

this as a random scatter of both sexes and children—in fact the local village cemetery for a number of generations. In contrast one might consider the Westerhus Mediaeval cemetery (Fig. 7), where there is clear regional bias of the sexes, so that had only part of the cemetery been excavated, a very distorted sex-ratio would have resulted.

Often of course, we can suggest reasons for unusual sex ratios. Referring back to the previous scatter diagram (Fig. 5), group 18 is from a Roman cemetery in York, the preponderance of males probably being explained by the fact that York was then an important garrison town, and a colonia where veterans might well have been settled in numbers (Warwick, 1962). Group 11 is an Early Christian Irish series from Gallen Priory (Howells, 1941), and what 12 females were doing mixed with 136 monks must remain a matter for pleasant conjecture! Group 14 was originally thought to consist of normal Saxon burials, but various evidence now points to the individuals being Mediaeval gallows victims. A final example; in Group 31, which is pooled material from nearby Iroquois ossuaries in Ontario, predominance of females has been tentatively explained

I

Children

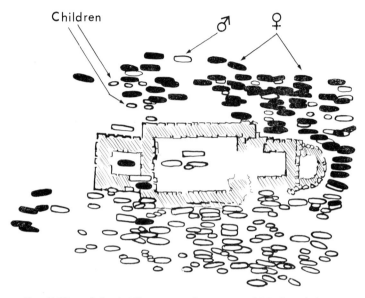

FIG. 7. Plan of the totally excavated cemetery of Mediaeval date, at Westerhus in Sweden (Gejvall, 1960). The segregation of males and females is clearly indicated. Small graves are of children.

as being due to the failure of war or raiding parties in retrieving all their dead (Churcher and Kenyon, 1960).

Did the proportion of the sexes vary in past groups relative to age? Figure 8 shows the relationships of the two sexes during seven age periods, in two ancient and two recent populations. Percentages are given for each sex, rather than the use of one sex ratio, so that we can at the same time keep in view the proportions of deaths occurring at a particular age period. It will be seen that the recent and early series display various differences, and in particular in the fluctuation in the preponderance of females. To some extent these are no doubt a function of sample size, but not completely, and in the Indian Knoll, Kentucky, series (a total of 452 adult skeletons) the puzzling reduction in females in the 25–39 year period is well marked. In contrast to these findings Chiarelli, et al. (1966) provide further variation in an early Egyptian series, and they have shown a maximum female peak in the 20–30 year old period, and relate it to the increased hazards of child-bearing during that age group. Clearly this is all worth further study.

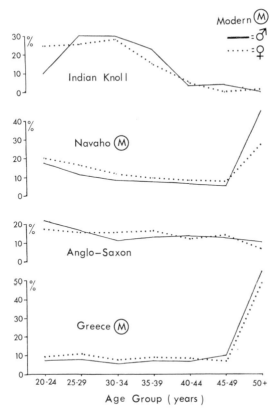

FIG. 8. Mortality differences between the sexes over the adult age periods, given in percentages. Two ancient (Indian Knoll, Anglo-Saxon) series, and two modern populations are given for comparison.

Health Status and Population

Howells (1960) has expressed some doubt as to whether special evidence of disease will ever be related to other aspects of early population demography. Of course to some extent this is true, and the detailed health analyses encompassed in modern demography are out of the question for ancient groups. But nevertheless, it would seem possible that some general trends in disease progress might be fruitfully explored. Without going into detail, let me just illustrate this point by reference to a specific example. Tuberculosis of the spine usually results in a well defined process of bone collapse, and kyphotic deformity. If this anomaly occurs more than rarely in a population then it is far more likely to be this than any other disease (even though other conditions occasionally mimic Pott's deformity). Now, if we plot cases of this spinal pathology as found in the early skeletal remains of Europe and Egypt, we get an interesting spacial separation related to the dating of the specimens (Fig. 9). The earliest cases are all from Egypt and Nubia, except for one possible example in Germany. By Mediaeval times, however, the examples have noticeably spread through northern Europe, and there are

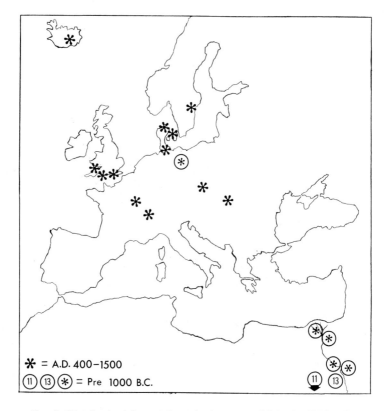

✱ = A.D. 400–1500

⑪ ⑬ ⊛ = Pre 1000 B.C.

Fig. 9. Distribution of cases of vertebral osteomyelitis in the Old World, probably indicative of tuberculosis. Two broad divisions of date are indicated. The distribution pattern of the more recent spinal pathology cases suggests a late establishment of the disease in Northern Europe. Encircled numbers refer to numbers of specimens with the condition in parts of Nubia.

sufficient cases (relative to the total skeletal numbers examined) to suggest very tentatively that tuberculosis had become a serious health threat in Europe by Saxon/Mediaeval times.

But in any case, I think the more we find out generally about the health status of these early communities, the more sense the related vital statistics will make. It is satisfactory that, with the growing interest in Palaeodemography, there is also taking place a return of attention to Palaeopathology (as instanced, for example, by Jarcho, 1966; and Brothwell and Sandison, 1967).

Armed with more general knowledge of this kind, and especially fuller histories of major diseases such as tuberculosis, the treponematoses, malaria, leprosy and smallpox, then we may hope to get a more balanced view of the health status of earlier populations. As Cook (1947) has already well argued, we tend to consider survivorship in ancient peoples in the light of findings on modern primitive and underdeveloped communities, but these latter groups are so often doubtful choices, having been pushed by contact with, or pressures of, "civilization" into tolerating unusually heavy loads of infection, disturbances in economy, and gross overpopulation.

It is to be hoped that this survey shows that the study of earlier populations has its contribution to make to demography, and that the palaeodemographer has his own special set of problems.

Appendix

Numerical list of earlier populations referred to in the text or figures. Site, archaeological period, sample size, and author of each study are given.

(1) Naga-ed-dêr, Egypt. Predynastic. 776 bodies. Lythgoe (1965).

(2) Fonyód, Hungary. Mediaeval. 165 bodies. Nemeskéri, et al. (1963).

(3) Zalavár-Burg, Hungary. 9th–11th century A.D. 450 bodies. Nemeskéri and Harsányi (1959).

(4) Kérpuszta, Hungary. 10th–11th century A.D. 395 bodies. Nemeskéri and Harsányi (1959).

(5) Zalavár-Kapelle, Hungary. 11th–12th century A.D. 177 bodies. Nemeskéri and Harsányi (1959).

(6) Westerhus, Sweden. Mediaeval. c. 379 bodies. Gejvall (1960).

(7) Bled, Jugoslavia. Mediaeval. 203 bodies. Skerlj and Dolinar (1950).

(8) Group A sites, Nubia. Prehistoric. Total of 202 bodies. Elliot Smith and Wood Jones (1908).

(9) Group B sites, Nubia. Early Dynastic. Total of 498 bodies. Elliot Smith and Wood Jones (1908).

(10) Cannington, England. Dark Ages. 462 bodies. Unpublished data of D. R. Brothwell and Rosemary Power.

(11) Gallen Priory, Ireland. Mediaeval. 148 bodies. Howells (1941).

(12) Castleknock, Ireland. Early Christian. 320 bodies. McLoughlin (1950).

(13) Bidford-on-Avon, England. Saxon. 222 bodies. Brash, et al. (1935).

(14) Dunstable, England. ?Mediaeval. 63 bodies. Dingwall (1931).

(15) Lachish, Israel. Iron Age. 695 bodies. Risdon (1939).

(16) Various sites in Illinois, U.S.A. Pre-Columbian. 483 bodies. Brothwell (from published and unpublished sources).

(17) Indian Knoll, U.S.A. c. 3000 B.C. 1122 bodies. Johnston and Snow (1961), Stewart (1962).

(18) Trentholme Drive (York), England. Roman. 290 bodies. Warwick (1962).

(19) Pooled Neolithic, Britain. 170 bodies. Brothwell, unpublished (1965 estimate).

(20) Southern Sites, pooled, England. Saxon. 573 bodies. Brothwell, unpublished.

(21) C-group burials, Nubia. c. 2280–1560 B.C. 450 bodies. Batrawi (1935).

(22) Meroitic burials, Nubia. 300 B.C.–A.D. 360. 364 bodies. Batrawi (1935).

(23) A-group burials, Nubia. c. 3500–2700 B.C. 180 bodies. Batrawi (1935).

(24) Grotte de Baye, France. Neolithic. 242 bodies. Ferembach (1964).

(25) Nebraska sites DK13, CD4, CD7, U.S.A. Protohistoric. 460 bodies. Bass (196).

(26) Zaculeu, Guatemala. Prehistoric. Sample of 219 bodies. Stewart (1963).

(27) Clopton, England. Mediaeval. 101 bodies. Unpublished data kindly provided by Mr. I. Tattersall.

(28) Lerna, Greece. Middle Bronze Age. 230 bodies. Angel (in Howells) (1960).

(29) Khirokitia, Cyprus. Neolithic. 178 bodies. Angel (1953).

(30) Pooled sites, North Africa. Ibero-Maurusian. 163 bodies. Vallois (1960).

(31) Tabor Hill (Ontario), Canada. c. A.D. 1200. 213 bodies. Churcher and Kenyon (1960).

References

ACSADI, G., NEMESKÉRI, J. and HARSÁNYI, L. (1959) Analyse des trouvailles anthropologiques du cimetiere de Kerpuszta (XIᵉ siècle) sous l'aspect de l'age (étude paleodemographique), Acta Archaeo. Acad. Sci. Hung. **11**, 419.

ANGEL, J. L. (1947) The length of life in Ancient Greece, J. Gerontol. **2**, 18.

ANGEL, J. L. (1953) The human remains from Khirokitia, Khirokitia, edited by P. Dikaios, Oxford University Press.

ANGEL, J, L, (1954) Human biology, health and history in Greece from first settlement until now, Year Book Am. Philo. Soc. pp. 168–174.

ARMELAGOS, C. J. (1965) Palaeopathology of sites from three archaeological horizons in Susanese Nubia. In press.

BARTELS, P. (1907) Tuberkulose (Wirbelkaries) in der jungeren Steinzeit, Arch. Anthrop. **6**, 243.

BASS, W. M. (1961) A preliminary survey of human skeletal material from archaeological sites in Nebraska, Plains Anthrop. **6**, 108.

BATRAWI, A. M. (1935) Report on the human remains, Mission Archeologique de Nubie 1929–1934, Government Press, Cairo.

BOYDE, A. (1963) Estimation of age at death of young human skeletal remains from incremental lines in the dental enamel, Third International Meeting in Forensic Immunology, Medicine, Pathology & Toxicology, London (unpublished).

BRASH, J. C., LAYARD, D. and YOUNG, M. (1935) The Anglo-Saxon skulls from Bidford-on-Avon, Warwickshire, and Burwell, Cambridgeshire, Biometrika **27**, 373.

BROTHWELL, D. and SANDISON, A. T. (Eds) (1965) Diseases in Antiquity, Thomas, Springfield.

BULLEN, A. K. (1963) Physical anthropology of the Goodman Mound, McCormack Site Duval County, Florida, Contributions of the Florida State Museum, Social Sciences, No. 10, 61.

CHIARELLI, B., MASALI, M. and DAVIDE, D. (1966) Ricerche sulk collezioni antropologiche egiziane dall' Istituto di Antropologia di Torino. II. Dati demografici sugli adulti, Riv. Anthrop. **53**, 1.

CHURCHER, C. S. and KENYON, W. A. (1960) The Tabor Hill ossuaries: a study in Iroquois demography, Hum. Biol. **32**, 249.

COOK, S. F. (1947) Survivorship in aboriginal populations, Hum. Biol. **19**, 83.

COON, C. S. (1959) Race and ecology in man, Cold Spring Harb. Symp. quant. Biol. **24**, 153.

DEEVEY, E. S. (1960) The human population, Scient. Am. **203**, 194.

DINGWALL, D. (1931) A barrow at Dunstable, Bedfordshire. Part II. The skeletal material, *Archaeol. J.* **88**, 210.

DOBYNS, H. F. (1966) Estimating aboriginal American population. I. An appraisal of techniques with a new hemispheric estimate, *Current Anthrop.* **7**, 395.

DUBLIN, L. I., LOTKA, A. J. and SPIEGELMAN, M. (1949) *Length of Life. A Study of the Life Table*, Ronald Press, New York.

ELLIOT SMITH, G. and WOOD JONES, F. (1908) The anatomical report, *Archaeological Survey of Nubia, Bull.* **2**, 29.

FEREMBACH, D. (1964) La masculinite (sex-ratio) chez les hommes modernes et chez les hommes fossiles, *Anthropologie* **1**, 27.

FRANZ, L. and WINKLER, W. (1936) Die Sterblichkeit in der fruhen Bronzezeit Niederosterreichs, *Z. Rassenk.* **4**, 157.

GEJVALL, N. G. (1960) *Westerhus. Medieval Population and Church in the Light of Skeletal Remains*, Ohlssons, Lund.

GENOVES, S. (1963) Estimation of age and mortality, *Science in Archaeology*, edited by D. R. Brothwell and E. S. Higgs, pp. 353–364, Thames and Hudson, London.

GOLDSTEIN, M. S. (1953) Some vital statistics based on skeletal material, *Hum. Biol.* **25**, 3.

HENSCHEN, F. (1966) *The History of Diseases*, Longmans, London.

HOWELLS, W. W. (1941) The Early Christian Irish: The skeletons at Gallen Priory, *Proc. R. Irish Acad.* **46**, 103.

HOWELLS, W. W. (1960) Estimating population numbers through archaeological and skeletal remains, *The Application of Quantitative Methods in Archaeology*, edited by R. F. Heizer and S. F. Cook, pp. 158–185, Viking Fund Publications in Anthropology, New York.

JAFFE, A. J. (1947) Notes on the rates of growth of the Chinese population, *Hum. Biol.* **19**, 1.

JARCHO, S. (Ed.) (1966) *Human Palaeopathology*, Yale University Press, New Haven.

JOHNSTON, D. F. (1966) An analysis of sources of information on the population of the Navaho, *Bull. Bur. Am. Ethnol.*, No. 197, Washington.

JOHNSTON, F. E. and SNOW, C. E. (1961) The reassessment of the age and sex of the Indian Knoll skeletal population: demographic and methodological aspects, *Am. J. Phys. Anthrop.* **19**, 237.

KERLEY, E. R. (1965) The microscopic determination of age in human bone, *Am. J. Phys. Anthrop.* **23**, 149.

KOBAYASHI, K. (1967) Trend in the length of life based on human skeletons from prehistoric to modern times in Japan, *J. Fac. Sci. Tokyo Univ.* (Sect. V), **3**, 108.

KURTH, G. (1963) Nyare naturvetenskapliga aspekter pa människans historia, *Ymer* **1**, 20.

LESLIE, V. (1953) Indian longevity, *West Virginia Archaeologist*, No. 6, 3.

LEWIS, T. M. N. and KNEBERG, M. (1946) *Hiwassee Island*. Quoted by Leslie (1953).

LISOWSKI, F. P., ASHTON, F. and ORMEROD, J. (1957) The skeletal remains from the 1952 excavations at Jericho, *Z. Morph. Anthrop.* **48**, 126.

LYTHGOE, A. M. (1965) *The Predynastic Cemetery N7000, Naga-ed-Dêr*, Part IV, University of California Press, Berkeley.

MACDONELL, W. R. (1913) On the expectation of life in Ancient Rome, and in the provinces of Hispania and Lusitania, and Africa, *Biometrika* **9**, 366.

McLoughlin, E. P. (1950) *Report on the Anatomical Investigation of the Skeletal Remains Unearthed at Castleknock in the Excavation of an Early Christian Cemetery in the Summer of 1938*, Stationery Office, Dublin.

Møller-Christensen, V. (1958) *Bogen om Aebelholt Kloster*, Dansk Videnskabs Forlag, Copenhagen.

Morel, P. and Demetz, J. L. (1961) *Pathologie Osseuse du Haut Moyen-Age*, Masson, Paris.

Morse, D., Brothwell, D. and Ucko, P. J. (1964) Tuberculosis in Ancient Egypt, *Am. Rev. Resp. Dis.* **90**, 524.

Nemeskéri, J. and Harsányi, L. (1959) Die bedeutung palaopathologischer untersuchungen fur die historische anthropologie, *Homo*, **10**, 203.

Nemeskéri, J., *et al.* (1963) Die Spatmittelalterliche bevolkerung von Fonyod, *Anthrop. Hung.* **6**, 1.

Pearl, R. and Gould, S. A. (1936) World population growth, *Hum. Biol.* **8**, 399.

Pearson, K. (1902) On the change in expectation of life in man during a period of circa 2000 years, *Biometrika* **1**, 261.

Risdon, D. L. (1939) A study of the cranial and other human remains from Palestine excavated at Tell Duweir (Lachish) by the Wellcome-Marston Archaeological Research Expedition, *Biometrika* **31**, 99.

Schaeffer, U. (1955) Demographische Beobachtungen an der Wikenger zeitlichen Bevolkerung von Haithabu, und Mittellung einiger pathologischer Befunde und den Skeletten, *Z. Morph. Anthrop.* **47**, 221.

Schultz, A. H. (1960) Age changes in primates and their modification in Man, *Human Growth*, edited by J. M. Tanner, Pergamon, London.

Schwartz, D. W. (1956) Demographic changes in the Early Periods of Cohinina prehistory, *Publs Anthrop. Viking Fund* **23**, 26.

Senyurek, M. (1957) The duration of life of the Chalcolithic and Copper Age populations of Anatolia, *Anatolia* **2**, 95.

Skerlj, B. and Dolinar, Z. (1950) Staroslovanska okostja z Bleda, *Slovene Academy of Sciences and Arts, Archeological and Anthropological Report for 1948*, Ljubljana, 67–103.

Stewart, T. D. (1953) Skeletal remains from Zaculeu, Guatemala, *The Ruins of Zaculeu, Guatemala*, edited by R. B. Woodbury and A. S. Trik, pp. 295–311, Byrd, Richmond.

Stewart, T. D. (1962) Comments on the reassessment of the Indian Knoll skeletons, *Am. J. Phys. Anthrop.* **20**, 1.

Stloukal, M. (1963) První pohřebiště na hradišti "valy" u Mikulčic, *Památky Archeologické* **56**, 124.

Thompson, J. E. S. (1967) The Maya central area at the Spanish Conquest and later: a problem in demography, *Proc. R. anthrop. Inst.* pp. 23–37.

Turner, C. G. and Lofgren, L. (1966) Household size of prehistoric western Pueblo Indians, *Southw. J. Anthrop.* **22**, 117.

Valaoras, V. G. (1936) A comparative study of the mortality of the population of Greece, *Hum. Biol.* **8**, 553.

Vallois, H. V. (1960) Vital statistics in prehistoric populations as determined from archaeological data, *The Application of Quantitative Methods in Archaeology*, edited by R. F. Heizer and S. F. Cook, pp. 181–222, Viking Fund Publications in Anthropology, New York.

Vyhnanek, L., Stloukal, M. and Kolar, J. (1967) Pathologische knochenbefunde im historischen material als quelle einer enganzenden populationscharakteristik, *Archeol. Rozhl.* **19**, 368.

WARWICK, R. (1962) The skeletons from the Trentholme Drive Cemetery, *Eburacum. Roman York*, pp. 109–110, H.M.S.O., London.
WILLEY, G. R. (1956) Problems concerning prehistoric settlement patterns in the Maya Lowlands, *Publs Anthrop. Viking Fund* **23**, 107.

HUMAN POPULATION DYNAMICS CONSIDERED FROM AN ECOLOGICAL STANDPOINT

J. G. SKELLAM

The Nature Conservancy, London, England*

Methodological Introduction

Modern philosophers of scientific method, despite their manifold differences, appear to adopt in some form or other what Reichenbach (1951) has called "the functional conception of knowledge". From a penetrating analysis of the logical structure of scientific statements, Wittgenstein and members of the Vienna Circle have gone so far as to regard a theory as *nothing but* an instrument for prediction. Even Popper (1959), despite his preoccupation with the relationships connecting prediction with verifiability and falsifiability rather than with application, nevertheless writes:

"Theories are nets cast to catch what we call 'the world': to rationalize, to explain, *and to master it.*"

Such in essence is the response of modern analytical philosophy to the age-old problem posed by Bacon in his *Novum Organum* when he said: "I would address one general admonition to all: that they consider what are the true ends of knowledge."

As we step down from the ivory towers of philosophy to the world of so-called practical men for whom past experience is irrelevant except as a guide to action, it is ironical to find not a single university chair established for the systematic study of the future, nor a single reputable scientific journal specifically dedicated to the subject.

In contrast to the apparently intelligent and purposeful behaviour of individual human beings, each operating in his own restricted

* The author is solely responsible for the views expressed. This article is not an official statement of the collective opinion of The Nature Conservancy.

spatio-temporal sphere of action, the human race considered as a collective entity rushes frantically on with increasing momentum in a kaleidoscopic world with no clear vision of possible dangers lying ahead and with no appropriately constructed inbuilt cybernetic mechanisms at present capable of correcting either the rate or direction of change.

The difficulties and pitfalls associated with extrapolation are well known, particularly in the field of human affairs, where the creative genius of highly gifted individuals and the decisions of men in authority are constant sources of novelty and surprise. As H. A. L. Fisher (1935) remarks in the Preface to his *History of Europe*:

"Men wiser and more learned than I have discerned in history a plot, a rhythm, a predetermined pattern. These harmonies are concealed from me. I can see only one emergency following another as wave follows upon wave, . . . and only one safe rule for the historian: that he should recognize in the diversity of human destinies the play of the contingent and the unforeseen."

Even so, much depends on the level of abstraction which we adopt. In Fig. 1, for example, which deals with a class of inventions, the envelope of the component curves may not be entirely beyond mathematical description.

It is quite understandable that workers in the human sciences should seem reluctant to sketch, even in broad outlines only, what appear to them to be plausible pictures of the next 50 years. Nevertheless, any such reluctance is open to three main types of interpretation. It is either (1) a tacit admission of their ignorance, bewilderment or incompetence, or (2) an expression of their complacency, indifference, escapism, or high-minded objective scientific detachment, or (3) a recognition of their impotence to influence the course of events.

Those scientific workers who fondly imagine that the foundations of logic and scientific method have been established for all time do not always appreciate that objectivity is a highly artificial attitude, difficult to maintain even in the realms of atomic physics. Complete objectivity is only possible when the intrinsic behaviour of the system being studied is totally unaffected both by the manner in which it is observed and by the knowledge which the investigator acquires about it. When the subject matter for study is itself human activity, any consistent attempt to regard scientific method as objective leads ultimately to the absurd requirement that the development of

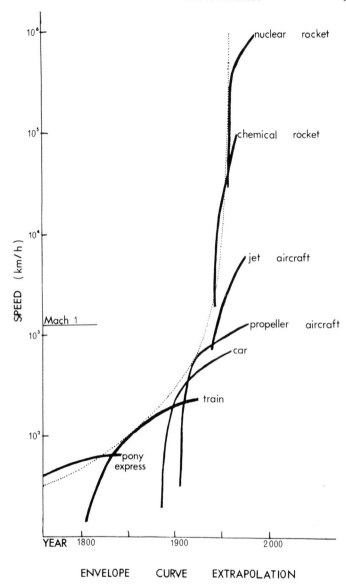

ENVELOPE CURVE EXTRAPOLATION

FIG. 1. To illustrate the feasibility of extrapolation in systems which are subject to innovation. After Jantsch (1967).

scientific methodology and the acquisition of scientific knowledge must both be disregarded as factors influencing the course of human affairs. It is however patently obvious that intellectual tools from the past do in fact profoundly affect the present behaviour of the system and that those we forge today will affect the system tomorrow.

It is evident that the current conception of the social function of science requires extension so as to include the understanding and control of the very changes which scientific discovery, acting in conjunction with man's basic instincts, has already unleashed. For after all, the behavioural make-up of man, forged by natural selection long before recorded history, has endowed present generations not only with an insatiable curiosity but also with a voracious appetite for immediate material satisfaction and with a ruthless capacity to exploit nature and their fellows (Morris, 1967). Despite the highly elaborate but nevertheless superficial division of labour displayed by this versatile, adaptable and gregarious anthropoid, a well coordinated social organization favouring extensive altruistic behaviour has not yet been evolved.

If the scientific investigation of the future of mankind is too colossal a task for single individual research workers, then it can only be tackled by organized co-operative effort. Man's latest tool is the electronic computer; his latest techniques are those of simulation and systems analysis linked to various optimization procedures already employed in operational research (Jantsch, 1967). Inadequate as present-day equipment might be for so gigantic a project, the first faltering steps must nevertheless be taken. Furthermore it must be recognized from the outset that the analytic, explanatory and diagnostic aspects cannot be sharply separated from the synthetic and prescriptive aspects based on an exploration of the full range of feasible alternative courses of action.

Population Growth and Food Potential

In recent years some bold attempts have been made to forecast the growth of the human population of the world up to the end of the century, notably by the United Nations Statistical Office, and to relate it to the world's actual and potential food supply. (Key references are given in the Bibliography.) The overall growth pattern which emerges is as shown in Fig. 2. The progressively increasing compound interest rate is a conspicuous feature. A recent estimate of the maximum theoretical biological productivity

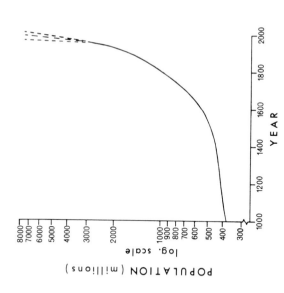

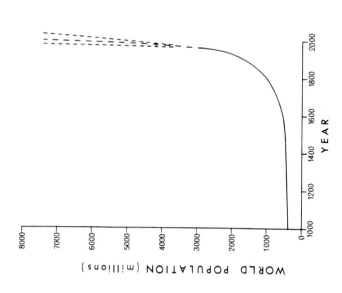

FIG. 2. The broad pattern of growth of the total human population of the world during the second millennium. After Revelle (1967).

$(19 \times 10^9$ tonnes of dry organic matter per year) and in particular of that fraction which is edible is shown in Fig. 3. A simple calculation, based on current consumption, indicates that food requirements will exceed the potential food supply in about 70 years at prevailing farming efficiencies [0·15 approx. on average] and in about 100 years if farming efficiencies could be doubled almost everywhere by markedly reducing pre- and post-harvest losses.

Mankind is clearly not only within sight of the realization of the biblical dream (*Hosea* 1) of multitudes "as the sand of the sea, which cannot be measured or numbered", but is also faced with the gloomy prospect of widespread disaster as envisaged by Thomas Malthus in 1789.

The population projections which have been published so far appear to be tinged with some of that buoyant confidence engendered by the wave of evolutionary utopianism which marked the turn of the century. It is, for example, commonly assumed that in the course of the next 35 years the underdeveloped parts of the world will become industrialized, and that as they mature their demographic history will parallel that of western countries at the corresponding phase of development, and in particular that the birth rate will decline. This is a whole complex of assumptions. Firstly, an extremely high population density is in itself a handicap to industrial development because human labour is then cheaper than machine labour and foreign exchange is used to import food rather than industrial plant. The situation is vastly different from that in Britain a century ago when the growing population (26 million) drew heavily on the produce of the soils of five continents and the surplus population freely emigrated to undeveloped territories overseas.

But even if industrial development were to proceed smoothly in the present underdeveloped regions of the world there would still remain a sharp contrast between western and non-western morals and traditions particularly in attitudes to sex, marriage and reproduction. There is therefore no guarantee that a raising of living standards would automatically suppress the birth rate. Indeed, in a recent survey mentioned by Revelle (1967), the number of children actually desired by couples in underdeveloped countries averaged 4 children per couple, which, with prospective levels of mortality, would lead to a doubling of population every 30 to 35 years. Voluntary birth control scarcely begins to operate until the family size which is desired is actually attained.

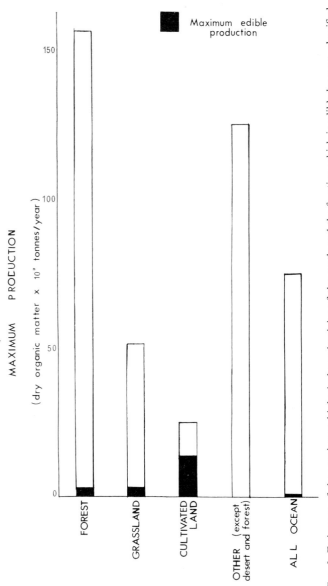

FIG. 3. Estimates of the maximum biological productivity of the earth and the fraction which is edible by man, classified under broad habitat types. After Ayres (1967).

K

Growth in a Heterogeneous System

In discussions on the growth of the world population there is a tendency to overlook a purely mathematical aspect which applies to growth rates in all heterogeneous systems, namely, that growth is ultimately dominated by the most rapidly growing component, and that under constant conditions the overall compound interest growth rate necessarily increases.

With the sole purpose of sharpening our ideas on this point and rationalizing our thinking, consider a simple two-compartment model constituted according to the present populations of the underdeveloped and developed parts of the world (i.e. in the ratio 2 : 1) and to which are allotted compound interest growth rates (in the ratio 5 : 2) comparable to those now envisaged. It is then easy to show that the overall growth rate can only be held down to the initial value by permitting a transfer of population from the larger compartment to the smaller (i.e. effecting a permanent change of growth status) on a scale approximately equal to the absolute rate of increase of the smaller compartment.

Ironically enough, even at low levels of migration, natural selection now operates strongly against the genotypes of peoples of the so-called "higher culture", whilst with unrestricted migration those genetic stocks which are now exposed to poverty and hardship would soon inherit the earth.

The Interaction of Ecological Components

A further reason for disquiet is the widespread prevalence of an optimistic conception of the balance of nature dating back to classical antiquity. In translation the relevant passage from Lucretius (*De Rerum Natura*) reads:

"At length everything is brought to its utmost limit of growth by nature, the creatress and perfectress. This is reached when that which is poured into its vital veins is no more than that which drains away. Here the growth of everything must halt. Here nature checks the increase of her own strength."

The impression created by this beautiful poetic passage is that of a steady monotonic approach to an asymptote, such as is described by the fruitful logistic law and other sigmoidal curves (Fig. 4).

When, however we study the simultaneous growth of interacting components, particularly where time-lags are involved, the approach

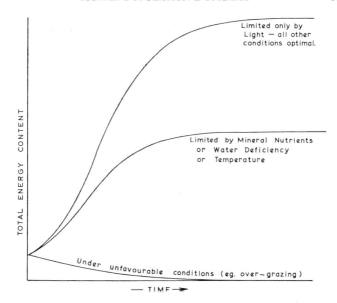

FIG. 4. The growth of a primary producer under various types of conditions.

to equilibrium is commonly oscillatory. Furthermore, the constant stream of environmental irregularity supplemented by chance happenings enhances vibration and tends to maintain the amplitude of the oscillations despite stabilizing forces, the general effect being somewhat similar to the swinging motion of a pendulum in the wind (Fig. 5).

Once again let us attempt to sharpen our thinking by considering a highly abstract producer–consumer system as illustrated in Fig. 6. In particular let us note that the physical transfer of "energy-laden" materials from the producer to the consumer reduces the productive capital of the former. In doing so it may or may not make the remaining capital more productive. This depends on the level to which the producer is already depressed and internal competition thereby reduced.

For any arbitrarily chosen fixed rate of transfer there is a critical level below which the productive capital cannot fall without suffering complete collapse (Fig. 7). Every biological productive system has its own maximum sustained yield which may be exceeded temporarily

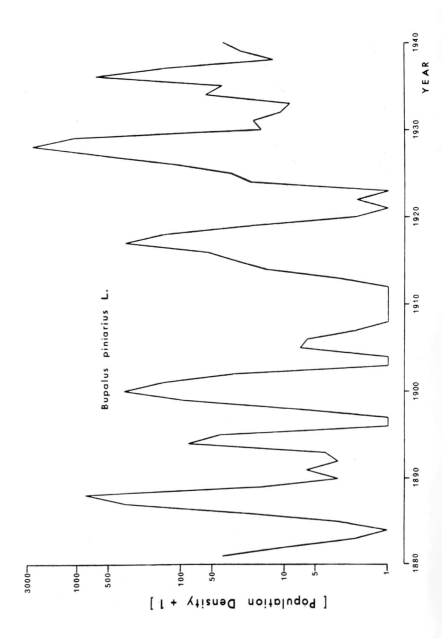

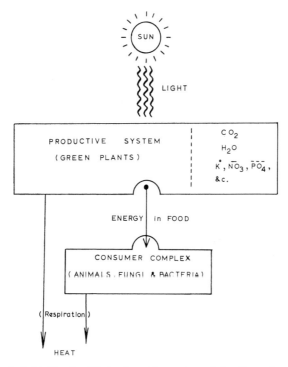

FIG. 6. A highly simplified schematic version of the flow of energy through an ecosystem.

but not indefinitely. Whether or not the productive system can recover when pressure is relaxed depends on its structure. Stocks of fish can and do recover from over-predation by man. Vegetation destroyed by over-grazing may not, for the underlying soil, the product of many hundreds of years of biological activity, becomes exposed to the elements, may be leached of its nutrients and eroded *en masse*. The plant–soil–climate complex is delicately balanced and liable to suffer a degenerative chain reaction if ever the pressure on it exceeds a critical value.

The course of change in a simple theoretical producer–consumer system is illustrated in Fig. 8, the pattern of behaviour being determined by the numerical values of the parameters of the system. A concrete example of a closely analogous interaction, the host–parasite relationship, is shown in Fig. 9. The fluctuation of the

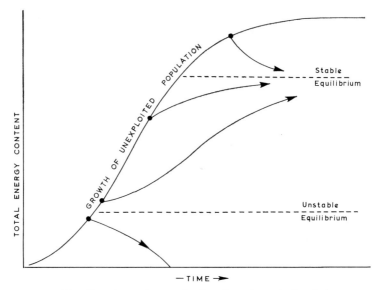

FIG. 7. The effect of cropping at a fixed moderate intensity in relation to the initial state of the exploited population.

consumer lags behind that of the producer by about a quarter of a period.

Man and his Habitat

The history of mankind likewise reveals some striking examples of the interaction between the consumer and the producer.

In the remote past when man lived as a hunter and food gatherer, his role in the natural ecosystem was perhaps not vastly different from that of many other large animals. Population levels were undoubtedly low, disease prevalent and starvation a frequent occurrence, as it still is in many parts of the world today.

At a later stage of development, early pastoralism and primitive agriculture made relatively minor demands on the fertility of the soil as a whole, at least for as long as the populations remained small and their economic and social organization simple.

In the course of development, human populations in certain centres rose and the surrounding land came under greater pressure. The removal of crops to feed the inhabitants of towns and cities tended

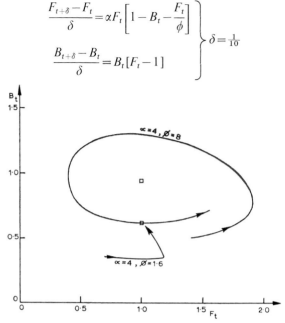

$$\frac{F_{t+\delta}-F_t}{\delta} = \alpha F_t\left[1 - B_t - \frac{F_t}{\phi}\right]$$

$$\frac{B_{t+\delta}-B_t}{\delta} = B_t[F_t - 1]$$

$$\delta = \frac{1}{10}$$

FIG. 8. To illustrate the two main types of behaviour possible in a producer–consumer system conceived on similar lines to the classical Volterra models. F_t and B_t denote the magnitudes at time t of the producer and consumer respectively. The passage of time is represented parametrically by the succession of points on the trajectory.

to rob the soil of its nutrients at a rate greater than their rate of replacement by natural processes. When, as a result, total biological productivity declined, the demand still remained, and pressures on the impoverished land were automatically intensified, thereby accelerating the degeneration of the soil often with profound disturbance to the normal water relations of the whole region.

There is indeed good reason to believe that unenlightened land management was a major factor leading to the collapse of Babylon and of Tyre, and that failure to maintain an adequate level of wheat production was one of the causes of the decline of the Roman Empire. Similarly, when in parts of the New World, the aboriginal population abandoned hunting and turned to agriculture, population densities mounted, and in such centres as Mexico exceeded the carrying capacity of the land. More was taken from the soil than

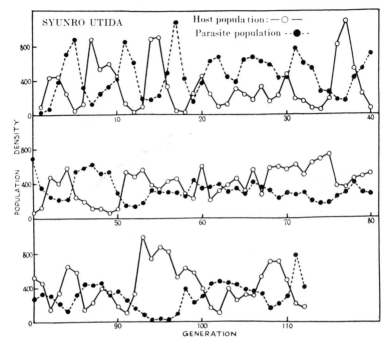

FIG. 9. The observed fluctuations in an experimental population maintained under uniform conditions over 112 generations. From Utida.

it could stand. More and more forest was destroyed; the last reservoir of soil fertility was thereby exploited and finally exhausted. Soil eroded, irrigation problems became insurmountable, and one by one the civilizations crumbled.

Throughout human history we find the same basic theme repeated with many variations—notably in the Mediterranean Region and the Middle East, and even in Highland Britain. The nitrate deposits of Chile and the guano deposits of Peru are already exhausted. The products from sewage disposal in urbanized areas compensate only for a small fraction of the soil nutrients being carried to the sea. The maintenance of soil fertility in the future is contingent not only on the expansion of the chemical industry, transport and the distribution of fertilizers, but also on the establishment and implementation of wise land management policies with long term objectives, able to resist the tempting short-term economic gains to be made out of the heavy demands for food-stuffs which mounting populations inevitably create.

Population Stability

The complete elucidation of the necessary and sufficient conditions for the stability of ecosystems is an elaborate technical problem. However, for any single insulated animal population, one simple necessary condition for equilibrium is that in the long run

$$\beta\lambda = 1,$$

where β is the crude birth rate (in the usual compound interest sense) and λ is the expectation of life from birth. Medical science and human motivation in conjunction have raised and are raising the value of λ in all parts of the world. As a result the human population, indeed the whole world ecosystem, is now in violent fundamental disequilibrium. The pure logic of the situation clearly reveals that if the value of β is not reduced then the value of λ must necessarily fall.

The longer that β remains at a level substantially greater than $1/\lambda$ the greater will be the ultimate impact on the habitat, the greater will be the danger of exceeding the maximum sustainable yield, and of the crash caused by the chain reaction which would inevitably follow. The greater too will be the pressures exerted by one local population on another and the perils and horrors which man's unparalleled aggressiveness might unleash. The statistical analysis of major human conflicts (Sutherland, 1962) almost suggests their inevitability under present conditions.

Concluding Remarks

The phenomenally rapid rise of *Homo sapiens* to ecological dominance marks only the beginning of a new ecological era which has yet to be established and sustained. In the words of H. A. L. Fisher (loc. cit.):

"The fact of progress is written plain and large on the page of history; *but progress is not a law of nature*. The ground gained by one generation may be lost by another. The thoughts of men may flow into channels which lead to disaster and barbarism."

From the cursory examination of man's role in the world ecosystem and the considerations outlined in this paper, it seems reasonable to conjecture that without an intellectual revolution, a new age of enlightenment, orientated to man's future and commensurate with the immensity of the problem, no satisfactory outcome to his present predicament can be envisaged.

References

AYRES, R. U. (1967) Food, *Sci. J., Lond.* **3**, 100–106.
BENJAMIN, B. (1962) World population trends, *Jl R. statist. Soc.* A, **125**, 378–386.
CALDER, RITCHIE (1962) The mathematics of hunger. *Jl R. statist. Soc.* A, **125**, 373–377.
FISHER, H. A. L. (1935) *History of Europe*, Eyre & Spottiswoode, London.
JANTSCH, E. (1967) Forecasting the future, *Sci. J., Lond.* **3**, 40–45.
MORRIS, D. (1967) *The Naked Ape*, Jonathan Cape, London.
PIRIE, N. W. (1962) Future sources of food supply: scientific problems, *Jl R. statist. Soc.* A, **125**, 399–417.
POPPER, K. R. (1959) *The Logic of Scientific Discovery*, Hutchinson & Co. Ltd., London.
REICHENBACH, H. (1951) *The Rise of Scientific Philosophy*, University of California Press, Berkeley and Los Angeles.
REVELLE, R. (1967) Population, *Sci. J., Lond.* **3**, 113–119.
SKELLAM, J. G. (1962) La Dynamique de la Population Humaine consideree du point de vue ecologique, *Entretiens de Monaco en Sciences Humaines*, 2ᵉ Session: 21–35. Hachette.
SUKHATME, P. V. (1961) The world's hunger and future needs in food supplies, *Jl R. statist. Soc.* A, **124**, 463–508.
SUTHERLAND, I. (1962) Statistics of human conflict, *Jl R. statist. Soc.* A, **125**, 473–483.
THOMAS, W. L. (Ed.) (1956) *Man's Role in Changing the Face of the Earth*, University of Chicago Press, Chicago.
UNITED NATIONS (1958) *The Future Growth of World Population*, U.N. Department of Economic & Social Affairs, New York.
VOGT, W. (1960) *Road to Survival*, William Sloane Associates, Inc., New York.

INTRAUTERINE GROWTH.
A DISCUSSION OF SOME OF THE
PROBLEMS BESETTING ITS
MEASUREMENT*

P. M. DUNN and N. R. BUTLER

Department of Child Health, University of Bristol

OUR knowledge of foetal growth is still meagre. If advances are to be made it is essential that we understand the reasons for our continuing ignorance and reach agreement as to the way in which the various outstanding problems may be tackled.

Until recently the foetus tended to fall between the obstetricians and the paediatricians, being comparatively neglected by both. Newborn infants were classified in groups according to their birth-weight. Prematurity was defined as a birth-weight of 2500 g or less and little attention was paid to the gestational age of the baby at delivery. Against such a background it is hardly surprising that progress was slow and that misconceptions flourished. Fortunately, these difficulties are now, for the most part, only a matter of historical interest.

Growth is a dynamic process with a rate which varies continuously throughout development. Therefore, to study this subject we must not only make serial records of the size and weight of the body but also be able to relate these measurements to the age of the infant. After birth these requirements present little difficulty; during prenatal life it is quite another matter. The inaccessibility of the foetus makes actual physical measurement impossible without delivery and termination of the pregnancy. It is true that serial data may be

* Based on a paper read to the Society for the Study of Human Biology, London, November 1967.

147

obtained using radiographic and ultrasonic techniques. However, the information is necessarily limited and often imprecise. If for the moment we discount these methods, we are left with such measurements as may be made at the time of birth. In theory, a single set of observations such as these can tell us nothing about pre-natal growth; in practice, we tacitly agree to regard the miniscule dimensions and mass of the fertilized ovum as uniform and negligible. Then, with a knowledge of the gestational age of the infant at the time of delivery, we can calculate the *mean* rate of growth throughout intra-uterine life. Unfortunately, the ascertainment of the gestational age presents many problems of its own. These must now be considered.

As we have no means of telling exactly when conception takes place, the practice has developed of calculating the gestational age from the first day of the last menstrual period (LMP). Although the best method available, it still has many potential sources of error. There may be menstrual irregularities or non-menstrual bleeding; alternatively the mother may give the date of the first missed period by mistake (Frazier, 1959) or she may deliberately mislead her doctor for social reasons. More commonly she may just fail to remember; this is hardly surprising in view of the high proportion of women who do not keep a written record of their menstrual history (Dunn, 1965), while, at the same time, half do not attend their doctor within the first four months of pregnancy (Butler and Bonham, 1963). In practice it is not unusual for about 7% of gestational calculations based on the LMP to be inaccurate by at least a month (Dunn, 1965).

While the problem just discussed will always be with us, there are ways in which we can ease it. First of all we must convince women of the importance of keeping an accurate menstrual record and of reporting at once to their doctor as soon as they have missed a period. Then, when they attend, we doctors must be most punctilious in questioning them and recording the relevant information. Even so there will, on occasions, be doubt as to the true date of the LMP. However, the size of the uterus during the second half of the first trimester provides a fairly reliable means of checking the cycle during which conception took place. Bi-manual palpation of the uterus should therefore be employed as a routine at this stage of pregnancy. Beyond the first trimester the size of the uterus varies too much for it to be of much value in determining the gestational age, though, with manual palpation of the foetus in the later weeks of pregnancy, it provides an approximate indication of the rate of intrauterine growth. The date of quickening is also worth recording but is likewise too variable to be used as more than a crude pointer to gestational age.

A second approach to this problem involves the use of various radiological, histological, biochemical and clinical techniques for estimating the maturity of the foetus during the last trimester of pregnancy and of the infant after delivery (Hartley, 1957; Engel and Butler, 1963; Mitchell and Farr, 1965; Brosens and Gordon, 1966; Levine *et al.*, 1966; Robinson, 1966). Unfortunately, all these methods have their disadvantages. Either they lack objectivity and depend too much on the experience and skill of the observer or they are insufficiently precise. In addition, there is the inevitable problem of evaluation because of the difficulty of obtaining reliable base-line information on foetal maturity. Therefore, while these new techniques have a real contribution to make to clinical practice and, taken together, provide a useful check on the validity of the mother's "dates", they cannot yet be used to establish gestational age *de novo*. If we are to learn more about foetal growth we must thus still rely primarily on base-line data recorded early in pregnancy respecting the LMP and the size of the uterus.

While in practice we calculate the gestational age from the date of the LMP, it is important to remember that ovulation usually takes place in mid-cycle, and that the conception age of the foetus is some two weeks less than the menstrual age. This would matter less if all menstrual cycles were of approximately the same length. In fact, at least a third of women have cycles lasting less than 25 or more than 30 days (Cox, 1968). McKeown *et al.* (1953) have produced some evidence to suggest that such differences are due mainly to variability of the pre-ovulatory phase of the cycle; if they are correct in thinking that the duration of the post-ovulatory phase is reasonably constant (14 days), then it becomes possible to "correct" the age of the foetus for variations in the length of the cycle provided that the latter are consistent. There still remains a need, however, for international agreement on these matters as well as on the units of time used to measure foetal age and the arbitrary divisions required to distinguish groups of infants born before, at, or after a "normal" length of gestation.

Problems of standardization extend also to the measurement of foetal size at birth though most workers now use the metric system and accept the W.H.O. (1961) recommendation with respect to birth-weight groups. Another problem must be mentioned. The fact that most infants are weighed at birth and comparatively few are measured externally has encouraged the practice of reporting and discussing foetal growth in terms of body weight alone. This is unsatisfactory as weight provides but a crude estimate of size or shape. It is influenced by the amount of fat and the degree of hydration of the infant as well as by the presence of a number of congenital anomalies. However, until more people have adopted the practice of measuring the infant at birth and reporting head circumference and length (Lubchenco *et al.*, 1966), we must do the best we can with the data which are available.

To recapitulate, we make single observations on each infant at birth and then, on the basis of experience with many infants delivered at different stages of gestation try to build up a picture of normal foetal growth. Unfortunately for our present purpose, normal infants are normally born at term; those born either before or after that time have frequently been associated with some complication of pregnancy capable of influencing foetal growth. In addition, groups of pre- and post-term infants tend to be loaded with cases in which mistakes have occurred in calculating the gestational age; this criticism applies particularly to many of the studies reported in the past in which data on foetal maturity was collected retro-spectively.

However, undeterred by these difficulties let us examine the data which have accumulated and the picture which has emerged of what we hopefully call normal foetal growth. How can this help us in the consideration of the individual infant? The most we can say is that he is either heavier or lighter, longer or shorter, or whatever, than other infants born at the same stage of gestation—and we can express this difference in terms of percentiles or in standard devia-tions from the mean. However, unless we know a great deal more about the many racial, genetic and environment variables that may have influenced this individual's growth *in utero*, as well as those of the population against which he is being compared, we can say little more. And if we did know all there was to know about these variables, we would still be limited to a knowledge of the infant's growth status at the moment of delivery. We can only guess as to the preceding pattern of growth in any particular case—though, with the aid of a good obstetrical history and a careful clinical examination this should not prevent us from guessing intelligently. Of course, many of these problems need not apply to laboratory investigations and already a considerable amount has been learnt from the study of animals such as monkeys whose conception and delivery has been planned (van Wagenen and Catchpole, 1965; Fujikura and Niemann, 1967).

We have mentioned the need for international standardization of the methods used to measure infant size and gestational age at birth. We must now discuss the need for agreement on yet a third standard based on both these parameters and representing birth-weight-for-gestation, or intra-uterine growth as it is often somewhat inaccurately called. In recent years there has been a population explosion in published "foetal growth" charts and this increase is likely to continue as the many variables influencing pre-natal growth are considered and reconsidered by different workers throughout the world. In the search for a general reference standard which can be used to compare these various studies and, at the same time, to detect with reasonable accuracy infants whose intra-uterine growth has deviated from the norm, arguments have been advanced in favour of accepting one or other of the charts based on a *specific* population. Before deciding whether this would be wise, let us pause to consider the qualities ideally required by such a reference standard.

First, if we wish to use our standard chart to study abnormal birth-weight-for-gestation, it ought itself to be based on *normal* foetal growth. Second, being intended for international use, the chart should be sufficiently flexible to take into account the normal variations, racial, genetic and environmental, which occur within and between different populations. Third, if we wish the standard to be widely used, it should be simple to understand, simple to remember and simple to reproduce.

Among the various foetal growth charts that have been considered for adoption as a universal standard, none have been more vigorously supported than that based on a study made in Denver, Colorado (Lubchenco et al., 1963; Battaglia and Lubchenco, 1967). Indeed, this chart is already widely used and has played a significant part in weaning obstetricians and paediatricians away from the old method of judging infant maturity at birth in terms of birth-weight alone. However, there are strong arguments against adopting this or any other chart based on a specific population as a reference standard.

Let us examine these reasons in relation to the Colorado chart. The Colorado chart (Fig. 1) was published in 1963. It was based on a study of the records of live-born infants of 24 to 42 weeks gestation born in, or, in the case of an unspecified number of pre-term infants, referred to a hospital in Denver between 1948 and 1961. After the arbitrary exclusion of certain groups of infants, the birth-weights-for-gestation of the remaining 5635 were graphed as percentiles and the curves smoothed arithmetically.

Now anyone who has struggled to gather reliable information on gestational age in *prospective* studies is likely to be worried about the

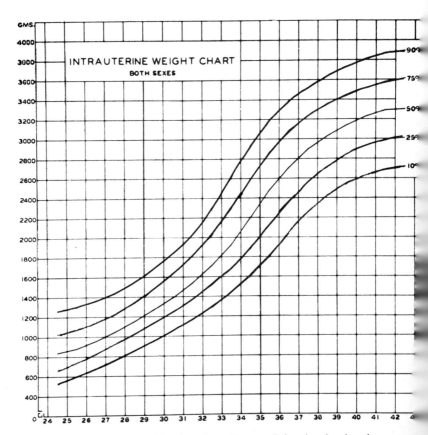

FIG. 1. The intra-uterine weight chart from Denver, Colorado, showing the percen distribution of birth-weight among live-born Caucasian infants at gestational ages fr 24 to 42 weeks (from Lubchenco *et al.*, 1963, by permission of *Pediatrics*).

validity of data obtained from records made up to 17 years before. Apart from this the Colorado chart lacks nearly all the qualities desirable in a reference standard. Based on the study of living hospital-born and referred infants, it does not even represent the population of Denver. Furthermore, there appear to be inconsistencies in the other criteria used to select cases. Why, for instance, should twins have been included in the study when infants of diabetic mothers were excluded? Why should infants whose birthweights seemed inappropriately small for their gestational age be accepted and those that appeared inappropriately large be arbitrarily rejected? And why were Negro, Oriental and Indian infants excluded from the sample and infants of Spanish, Mexican and American Indian extraction included?

Even more important than these considerations is the lack of available information respecting the operation, in the population under study, of the various socio-biologic factors known to influence intra-uterine growth. How, for instance, can we investigate the significance of maternal age, height, parity, nutrition, social class and smoking habits or the effect various maternal and foetal diseases have on intra-uterine growth if we do not know the extent to which these factors influenced the findings on which our standard reference chart is based? One fact we *do* know and it is far from reassuring. Denver is located some 5000 feet above sea-level. Lubchenco and her colleagues (1963) themselves suggest that this altitude may explain the fact that the median weight for their term infants was significantly lower than that reported for Caucasian infants in other studies made in the United States. Even greater differences exist in relation to pre-term infants. In 1966, Battaglia *et al.* compared the Colorado chart with their own findings in Baltimore and with those of a study made by Erhardt and his associates (1964) in New York. While they found reasonably close agreement between all three graphs after the 36th week of gestation, before that time there were striking differences between the Baltimore and New York studies, on the one hand, and the Colorado chart on the other. Thus, the birth-weight for infants on the 50th percentile of the Colorado chart at 32 weeks gestation was 1715 g, while that for the other two studies was approximately 2150 g; the figures for the 90th percentiles at the same stage of gestation were 2280 g and 3200 g (approx.) respectively. Such discrepancies surely speak for themselves.

L

In case these criticisms appear unduly harsh, we must hasten to add that the Colorado chart is certainly no "worse" than any of the many similar graphs that have been published. Indeed, over the last few years it has succeeded in stimulating important advances in this field. But it was not originally designed to serve as an international reference standard and progress would undoubtedly be impeded if it was forced into this rôle.

So much for criticism. It is less easy to produce a satisfactory alternative. We still badly need more and better data on the many normal and pathologic variables influencing pre-natal growth. Such information will not become available until large-scale studies have been made using multivariate analysis. The British Perinatal Mortality Survey (Butler and Bonham, 1963) makes a start in the right direction. In the second report, published in 1969, Butler and Alberman present data on the birth-weight-for-gestation of the 17,000 infants born in Britain during one week in March 1958. Many of the recognized variables influencing pre-natal growth have been studied individually and the results expressed in percentile form and also in standard deviations from the mean. Even more extensive studies are still required both here and in other countries with different racial, genetic and environmental backgrounds. Until such studies have been made, much of what we say on this subject is bound to be speculative. This should not deter us, however, from attempting to create a standard reference chart, even though we have to base it on incomplete and imperfect information. Our own tentative efforts in this direction will now be described.

Many years ago Yllpö (1919) and others showed that there was a linear relationship between birth-weight and gestational age throughout most of the second half of pregnancy. This observation has been repeatedly confirmed and has also been shown to apply to a number of other mammals including monkeys (van Wagenen and Catchpole, 1965). Only when term is approached or reached is there found to be a loss of linearity owing to a decrease in the incremental weight gain of the foetus.

In 1953, McKeown and Record observed that singleton infants, following their delivery, resumed the same linear rate of weight gain that had been present during most of the second half of pregnancy (Fig. 2). From this evidence they deduced that the reduction in the rate of growth of singleton foetuses at term was due to restrictions imposed by the intra-uterine environment. They also noted that a

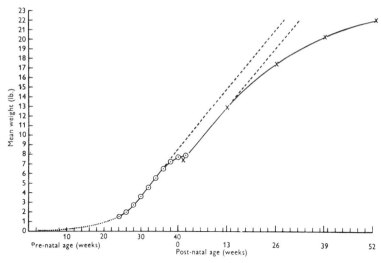

FIG. 2. Chart showing the pre- and post-natal weight gain of normal singleton infants. After delivery the infant resumes the linear weight gain present during the last trimester of pregnancy before the period of terminal constraint (from McKeown and Record, 1953, by permission of *J. Endocr.*).

reduction in the rate of growth determined by the foetus itself did not take place until some months after birth*.

McKeown and Record's work on multiple births is also of interest in this context. In 1952 they had shown that, as litter size increased, the terminal loss of linear weight gain took place progressively earlier (Fig. 3). The average mother that they studied appeared to be capable of supporting normal foetal growth in multiple pregnancy until the total litter weight reached about 7 lb. Thereafter the litter weight increment was approximately the same regardless of the size of the litter.

The results just discussed support the view that environmental factors in utero are responsible for the terminal decrease in the rate of foetal weight gain. We consider this hypothesis to be of crucial importance and make use of it in the construction of our reference chart. For, if we are to learn more about the influence of these environmental factors on growth, it is essential not to include them

* This is not strictly true since a linear gain in weight must represent a steady deceleration in the rate of growth (Dunn and Butler, 1968).

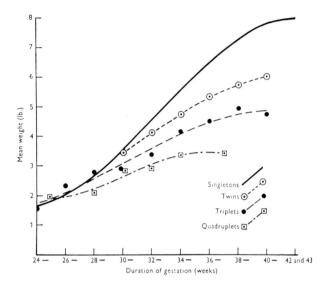

Fig. 3. Mean birth-weight-for-gestation curves of single and multiple foetuses during the second half of pregnancy (from McKeown and Record, 1952, by permission of *J. Endocr.*).

in our original standard. We believe that the latter should be based on the normal lineal growth velocity of the foetus. Gruenwald (1966) has made similar use of a straight line and has implied that a loss of linearity indicates constraint of growth.

But how are we to ascertain the slope and position of our line? Ideally we need reliable information on the birth-weights-for-gestation of healthy male and female singleton infants born throughout the last trimester of pregnancy to healthy well-nourished women in their twenties who are not primiparae and do not smoke. However, until such information is available, we must do the best we can with that which is. We argue thus. It is well recognized that the data for infants on the upper and lower percentiles of a birth-weight-for-gestation chart tend to be less reliable than that for those lying in between. At the same time we know that there is an increased perinatal morbidity and mortality among infants deviating much above or below the mean birth-weight at each gestational age. From this we may deduce that the optimum rate of growth (and, if one accepts Nature's law of survival, the normal rate of growth) is likely to lie near to or on the mean rate of growth for a population *during the period of unconstrained growth.*

With these considerations in mind we examined data on the mean birth-weight-for-gestation from our own studies as well as from those reported in the world literature. As constraint of foetal growth can be detected from the 37th week in the average singleton pregnancy, we should, strictly speaking, have confined our studies to data concerning infants delivered during the first 9 weeks of the last trimester. However, as has been noted, the information on babies born at term tends to be more reliable than that for those born earlier. In addition, the loss of linearity in most studies between the 37th and 40th weeks is only small (Fig. 5). It thus seemed expedient and also reasonable to consider data from the whole 28- to 40-week period.

Because of the varying criteria that have been used to select cases and the lack of uniformity in the methods employed to report results, it was not possible to make more than a crude comparison of the information provided by different studies. In consequence, the line representing normal foetal growth, while relating as closely as possible to observed experience, must eventually be determined

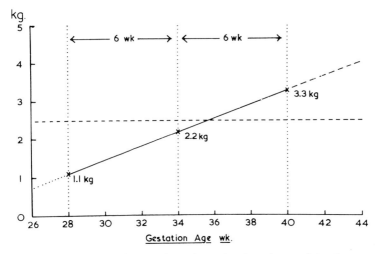

FIG. 4. Birth-weight-for-gestation chart showing the straight line selected to represent the mean unconstrained growth of the Caucasian infant (see text). The interrupted horizontal line at 2500 g was once used to define " prematurity".

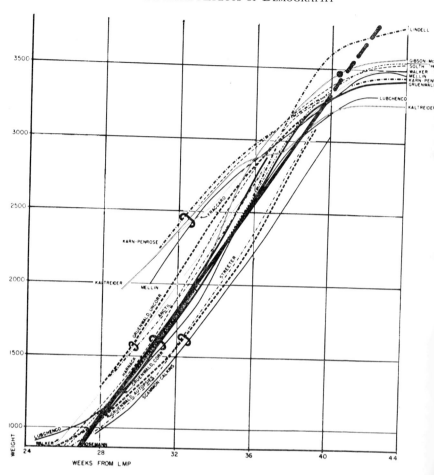

FIG. 5. The line selected to represent the mean unconstrained growth of the Caucasian foe (see Fig. 4) has been superimposed on a chart showing the mean birth-weight-for-gestat curves from a number of studies in the literature (adapted from Gruenwald, 1966, permission of *Am. J. Obstet. Gynec.*).

in an arbitrary fashion. After careful consideration we decided that the normal growth velocity of an average Caucasian foetus was best represented by a line drawn from a weight of 1·1 kg at 28 weeks, through 2·2 kg at 34 weeks, to 3·3 kg at 40 weeks and then extrapolated (Fig. 4). In Fig. 5 this line has been superimposed on a diagram from a paper by Gruenwald (1966) showing a number of birth-weight-for-gestation curves from the literature. It was of interest to find that our line passed through the "hoop" enclosing the curves that Gruenwald considered to be most representative of their respective populations. In addition, the basic measurements on which our line is based are very easy to remember while the line itself is, of course, extremely simple to reproduce. Nor is that all. If the line is extrapolated into post-natal life we obtain, successively, weights of 4·4 kg at 6 weeks, 5·5 kg at 12 weeks, 6·6 kg at 18 weeks and 7·7 kg at 24 weeks. In Fig. 6 this extrapolated line has been superimposed on charts showing the percentile weight distribution curves for boys and girls in Britain during the first year of life (Tanner, 1958). It will be seen how closely the former coincides with the median values of the latter during the first five months. This would appear to lend support to McKeown and Record's (1953) observation regarding the similarity of the velocity of unconstrained growth before birth with that taking place in the first few months of post-natal life. Finally, our line is endowed with yet another attribute which may prove most convenient. Any foetus having such a growth velocity doubles its weight (from 1·1 to 2·2 kg) during the first 6 weeks of the last trimester (Fig. 4). If we agree to call this amount of growth "100%", then that taking place during the second half of the last trimester (from 2·2 to 3·3 kg) is only half as great or "50%". During the three subsequent 6-week periods after birth, the amount of growth falls successively to "33%", "25%", and "20%" of its original level.

We believe that our sloping line representing mean Caucasian foetal growth is based on rational arguments and reasonably good evidence, and that it has considerable advantages over the "horizontal" weight lines recommended in the past (W.H.O., 1950) and still used by some workers today (Ghosh and Daga, 1967; Yerushalmy, 1967). It would be possible and, indeed, it might be wise to stop at this point; for, from here on, our hypothesis is on less sure ground. If we do continue, it is because such evidence as is available appears to support our ideas and because we believe that they may prove of real help in the study of this complex subject. At the worst they should serve to stimulate discussion.

During pregnancy, the human conceptus successively doubles its weight some 30 times in the process of developing from an ovum weighing approximately 0·005 mg to a fully grown foetus. If we define the rate of growth in terms of the time taken to double body weight, then we find that 95% of pre-natal growth occurs before the 28th week of gestation, 77% of it taking place during the first trimester. Although the rate of growth is comparatively slow during the later weeks of pregnancy, weight gain is, somewhat paradoxically, proceeding most rapidly at this time. This concept is illustrated in Fig. 7. It may be seen that very small deviations ($\mp$ 1–2%) in the velocity of growth throughout pregnancy are capable of accounting for the wide variation in birth-weight existing at term. In the past it has been suggested that the latter was due to the operation of varying degrees of intra-uterine constraint. We believe that, within narrow limits, true differences also exist between the normal growth velocity of one foetus and the next. This hypothesis receives support from the work of Fujikara and Niemann (1967) who found that the variability in the birth-weight of monkeys following timed matings was roughly constant regardless of the gestational age.

There can be no doubt that many pathological conditions affecting the mother and her conceptus are capable of constraining foetal growth early in pregnancy in a way similar to that in which it may be constrained at term. While eventually we wish to study this subject, at the present time we are more interested in determining the factors which regulate normal unconstrained growth. In this context the studies of Walton and Hammond (1938) on horses seem highly pertinent. They showed that the birth-weights of foals born to Shetland dams of Shire sires were closely similar to those of pure Shetlands. Likewise, the foals of Shire dams by Shetland sires were roughly the same weight as those of pure Shires. The work of Morton (1955) and Robson (1955) and, more recently, of Ounsted (1965, 1966) suggest that the growth of the human foetus is also regulated in a similar manner by its mother (Ounsted and Ounsted, 1966). Indeed, it is not unlikely that this maternal regulation determines and accounts for a considerable part of the observed range in birth-weight between and within different races. Considering the narrow limits of tolerance between the size of the mother's birth canal and that of the foetus at term, such an arrangement would obviously be advantageous. Thus, it is hardly surprising to find that the mean birth-weight of infants born to the tall, well-built Swedes (3600 g) is some 1000 g or 37% greater than that for the infants of the diminutive Ngayu pigmy (2573 g) (Lindell, 1956; Vincent et al., 1962).

The growth of the foetus also appears to be influenced by its own genetic make-up, though to a much lesser degree. For instance, it is recognized that the mean birth-weight-for-gestation of boys throughout the last trimester is significantly greater than that of girls (Gibson and McKeown, 1952); and this difference is continued into post-natal life (Fig. 6).

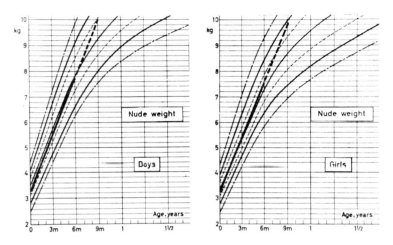

FIG. 6. The line selected to represent the mean unconstrained growth of the Caucasian foetus has been extrapolated and superimposed on Tanner and Whitehouse weight charts for boys and girls during the first year of post-natal life. There is a close correspondence between the former and the two post-natal charts during the first 6 months of life (adapted from Tanner, 1968).

Because the foetal growth velocity varies within such narrow limits and because 95% of foetal growth (as defined earlier) takes place during the first 28 weeks of pregnancy, we can afford to assume that, for practical purposes, all foetuses have the same *potential* growth velocity during the last trimester and differ only in their initial weight at 28 weeks' gestation. Let us put it another way. Within any population there must be sub-groups, as, for example, males and females, with the same growth velocity but with birth-weights-for-gestation that are balanced evenly above and below the mean for the whole group. Uninfluenced by constraint, these subsidiary birth-weight "curves" will not lie parallel to the mean "curve" but will progressively diverge away from it and from each other, like neighbouring spokes in a wheel. Now our original line representing the mean growth velocity of the Caucasian foetus was drawn from a weight of 1·1 kg at 28 weeks to 3·3 kg at 40 weeks. If we apply the principle that we have just discussed to it, then we can construct a whole series of diverging lines that relate to the original line in that they also demonstrate a "tripling" of foetal weight during the last trimester of pregnancy.

Fig. 8 shows a chart, which we have called the Gestogram, that has been constructed in the manner just described. The upper and lowermost lines have been drawn from weights of 1·5 and 0·7 kg at 28 weeks to 4·5 and 2·1 kg at 40 weeks. Alternatively, this might be expressed as 1·1 kg ± 0·4 at 28 weeks to 3·3 kg ± 1·2 at 40 weeks, or even more simply in terms of our original line plus or minus 36·4%. The intermediate lines in the diagram represent the original line plus or minus 18·2%. At this point we must simplify our terminology. Each foetal growth line, to be referred to as FGL for short, will be distinguished by the weight shown on it at 40 weeks. Thus, our original line becomes "FGL 3·3 kg".

The Gestogram covers fairly generously the area throughout which the birth-weight-for-gestation of the human infant is normally distributed. Of course, any number of FG lines might be drawn. In

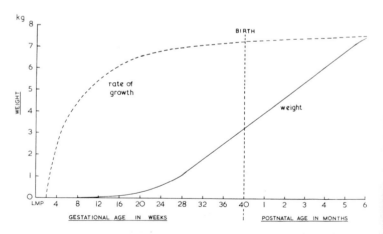

FIG. 7. Chart showing the weight gain (———) and rate of growth (– – – –) (see text for definition) during pre-natal and the first 6 months of post-natal life. Weight gain is greatest during the last trimester and after birth; paradoxically, the rate of growth is relatively slow at this time.

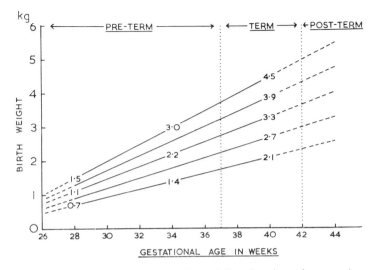

FIG. 8. The Gestogram—a scaffolding of lines based on the normal unconstrained growth velocity of the foetus (see text).

practice we have often found it convenient to use the intermediate FG lines 2·4, 3·0, 3·6 and 4·2 kg in addition to those shown in Fig. 8. When this is done, each FGL at term will be found to be separated from its neighbour by 0·3 kg; at 28 weeks, the lines are separated by intervals of 0·1 kg.

We must now consider the uses to which the Gestogram may be put. First, it may serve as a convenient and arbitrary way of dividing up groups of infants weighing more or less than the average. In the case of Caucasian populations the "FGL 3·3 kg" may be used, of course, to represent the mean. Second, if our various assumptions are correct, it may be used to compare and study groups of infants with different mean FG lines. Let us suppose, for example, that the FGL of the Swedish foetus is 3·6 kg and that of the Belgian Congo pigmy 2·7 kg. It now becomes possible to make direct comparisons between these two racial groups. Thus, if we wish to compare the constraining influence of maternal smoking on foetal growth in each population, we can do so in terms of the percentage deviation from each respective FG line. In passing, it is worth noting that an infant with an FGL of 2·7 kg gains exactly 150 g in weight each week, while one with an FGL of 3·6 kg gains 200 g per week.

A third advantage of the Gestogram was revealed when it was used to compare the 90th and 10th percentile curves of the birth-weights-for-gestation of three predominantly Caucasian populations studied in Denver, in Baltimore, and in Newcastle (Lubchenco *et al.*, 1963; Battaglia *et al.*, 1966; Neligan, 1965). It was found that from the 37th to the 42nd week of gestation there was a remarkably close agreement between the three 90th percentiles and the "FGL 3·9 kg", on the one hand, and the three 10th percentiles and the "FGL 2·7 kg", on the other. Before the 37th week the various percentile curves deviated widely both from the FG lines and also from each other, providing yet a further reason for suspecting the reliability of the data on which these percentiles were based at this stage of gestation. Now, Battaglia and Lubchenco (1967) had suggested that the 90th and 10th percentile curves of the Denver chart may be used to separate infants of "appropriate" size for their gestational age from those

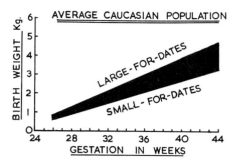

Fig. 9. Possible use of the Gestogram to define Caucasian infants that are inappropriately "large" or "small" for their gestational age at birth. The justification and limitations of this definition are discussed in the text.

that are either "large" or "small"; if such a distinction is indeed desirable, there seems no reason why the "FGL 3·9 kg" and "FGL 2·7 kg" should not serve equally well in this capacity for Caucasian populations (Fig. 9), at any rate with respect to term infants. Comparable limits of plus or minus 18·2% of the mean FGL could be used for other populations with mean FG lines greater or less than that characteristic of the Caucasian. Before leaving this subject, it must be emphasized that the FG lines are not themselves percentile curves and that more work is required, in particular with respect to pre-term infants, before the validity of the use to which they have tentatively been put in Fig. 9 can be verified.

In conclusion, we may say that we have tried to create a standard chart based on the normal growth velocity of the foetus. We believe that it is both simple to understand and simple to use, while at the same time it is versatile enough to permit study of the various racial, genetic and environmental factors (physiological and pathological) influencing pre-natal growth. The need for a standard foetal growth chart for international use is pressing (Amer. Acad. Pediat., 1967). While we make no claim that ours is perfect or that we can yet substantiate all the assumptions and hypotheses that have been used in its construction, we would suggest that its advantages are greater and its disadvantages fewer than those of its competitors, and that its use would be likely to clarify rather than to further confuse the murky situation existing at the present time.

Acknowledgement

One of us (P.M.D.) was supported by a research grant from the Van Neste Foundation.

References

AMER. ACAD. PEDIAT., COMMITTEE ON FETUS AND NEWBORN (1967) Nomenclature for duration of gestation, birth weight and intra-uterine growth, *Pediatrics* **39**, 935.

BATTAGLIA, F. C., FRAZIER, T. M. and HELLEGERS, A. E. (1966) Birth weight, gestational age, and pregnancy outcome, with special reference to high birth weight–low gestational age infant, *Pediatrics* **37**, 417.

BATTAGLIA, F. C. and LUBCHENCO, L. O. (1967) A practical classification of newborn infants by weight and gestational age, *J. Pediat.* **71**, 159.

BROSENS, I. and GORDON, H. (1966) The estimation of maturity by cytological examination of the liquor amnii, *J. Obstet. Gynaec. Br. Commonw.* **73**, 88.

BUTLER, N. R. and ALBERMAN, E. D. (1969) in Perinatal problems. The Second Report of the 1958 British Perinatal Mortality Survey, Livingstone, London.

BUTLER, N. R. and BONHAM, D. G. (1963) in Perinatal Mortality. The First Report of the 1958 British Perinatal Mortality Survey, Livingstone, London.

COX, H. J. E. (1968) Length of menstrual cycle, *Brit. med. J.* **1**, 252.

DUNN, P. M. (1965) The respiratory distress syndrome of the newborn: immaturity versus prematurity, *Archs. Dis. Childh.* **40**, 62.

ENGEL, R. and BUTLER, B. V. (1963) Appraisal of conceptual age of newborn infants by electroencephalographic methods, *J. Pediat.* **63**, 386.

ERHARDT, C. L., JOSHI, G. B., NELSON, F. G., KROLL, B. H. and WEINER, L. (1964) Influence of weight and gestation of perinatal and neonatal mortality by ethnic group, *Am. J. publ. Hlth* **54**, 1841.

FRAZIER, T. M. (1959) Error in reported data of last menstrual period, *Am. J. Obstet. Gynec.* **77**, 915.

FUJIKURA, T. and NIEMANN, W. H. (1967) Birth weight, gestational age, and type of delivery in rhesus monkeys, *Am. J. Obstet. Gynec.* **97**, 76.

GHOSH, S. and DAGA, S. (1967) Comparison of gestational age and weight as standards of prematurity, *J. Pediat.* **71**, 173.

GIBSON, J. R. and McKEOWN, T. (1952) Observations on all births (23,970) in Birmingham, 1947, *Br. J. soc. Med.* **6**, 152.

GRUENWALD, P. (1966) Growth of the human fetus. I. Normal growth and its variation, *Am. J. Obstet. Gynec.* **94**, 1112.

HARTLEY, J. B. (1957) Radiological estimation of foetal maturity, *Br. J. Radiol.* **30**, 561.

LEVINE, B., ELY, C. W., Jr and WOOD, W. A., Jr (1966) Assessment of fetal maturity by maternal serum alkaline phosphatase analysis, *Am. J. Obstet. Gynec.* **96**, 1155.

LINDELL, A. (1956) Prolonged pregnancy, *Acta obstet. gynec. scand.* **35**, 136.

LUBCHENCO, L. O., HANSMAN, C. and BOYD, E. (1966) Intrauterine growth in length and head circumference as estimated from live births at gestational ages from 26 to 42 weeks, *Pediatrics* **37**, 403.

LUBCHENCO, L. O., HANSMAN, C., DRESSLER, M. and BOYD, E. (1963) Intrauterine growth as estimated from liveborn birth-weight data at 24 to 42 weeks of gestation, *Pediatrics* **32**, 793.

McKEOWN, T., GIBSON, J. R. and DOUGRAY, T. (1953) Association between period of gestation and length of menstrual cycle, *Br. med. J.* **ii**, 253.

McKEOWN, T. and RECORD, R. G. (1952) Observations on foetal growth in multiple pregnancy in man, *J. Endocr.* **8**, 386.

McKEOWN, T. and RECORD, R. G. (1953) The influence of placental size on foetal growth in man, with special reference to multiple pregnancy, *J. Endocr.* **9**, 418.

MITCHELL, R. G. and FARR, V. (1965) The meaning of maturity and the assessment of maturity at birth. In: Gestational Age, Size and Maturity. *Clin. develop. Med.* No. 19, edited by M. J. R. Dawkins and W. G. MacGregor, Heinemann, London, p. 83.

MORTON, N. D. (1955) The inheritance of human birth weight, *Ann. hum. Genet.* **20**, 125.

NELIGAN, G. (1965) A community study of the relationship between birth weight and gestational age. In: Gestational Age, Size and Maturity, *Clin. develop. Med.* No. 19, edited by M. J. R. Dawkins and W. G. MacGregor, Heinemann, London, p. 28.

OUNSTED, M. (1965) Maternal constraint of foetal growth in man, *Develop. Med. Child Neurol.* **7**, 479.

OUNSTED, M. (1966) Unconstrained foetal growth in man, *Develop. Med. Child Neurol.* **8**, 3.

OUNSTED, M. and OUNSTED, C. (1966) Maternal regulation of intrauterine growth, *Nature, Lond.* **212**, 995.

ROBSON, E. B. (1955) Birth weight in cousins, *Ann. hum. Genet.* **19**, 262.

TANNER, J. M. (1958) in *Modern Trends in Paediatrics*, second series, edited by A. Holzel and J. M. P. Tizard, Butterworth, London.

VAN WAGENEN, G. and CATCHPOLE, H. R. (1965) Growth of the fetus and placenta of the monkey (*Macaca mulatta*), *Am. J. phys. Anthrop.* **23**, 23.

VINCENT, M., JANS, C. and GHESQUIERE, J. (1962) The newborn pigmy and his mother, *Am. J. phys. Anthrop.* **20**, 237.

WALTON, A. and HAMMOND, J. (1938) The maternal effects on growth and conformation in Shire horse–Shetland pony crosses, *Proc. R. Soc. B,* **125**, 311.

WORLD HEALTH ORGANIZATION EXPERT GROUP ON PREMATURITY (1950): final report. Geneva, Switzerland: W.H.O. Technical Report Series No. 27, 1950.

WORLD HEALTH ORGANIZATION, EXPERT COMMITTEE ON MATERNAL AND CHILD HEALTH: Public Health Aspects of Low Birth Weight (1961). W.H.O. Technical Report Series, Geneva, Switzerland: No. 217.

YERUSHALMY, J. (1967) Classification of newborn infants by birthweight and gestational age, *J. Pediat.* **71**, 164.

YLLPÖ, A. (1919) Zur physiogie, klinik und zum schicksal der fruhgeborenen, *Z. Kinderheilk.* **24**, 1.